LEGEND THAT YOU ARE

RECREATE THE STORY
OF YOUR LIFE

Janet Pearson

legend
THAT YOU ARE

on the
dragon's
side
PRODUCTIONS

KASLO, BC

For Kelly, Oceanna and Xandra
May your stories be rich and amazing.

Copyright © 2013 by Janet Pearson

Published by On the Dragon's Side Productions
Post Office Box 1396
Kaslo, BC Canada V0G 1M0
www.dragonsside.com

All rights reserved. This book may not be reproduced in whole or in part without written permission from the publisher, except by a reviewer who may quote brief passages in a review; nor may any part of this book be reproduced, stored in a retrieval system, or transmitted in any form or by any means, electronic, mechanical, photocopying, recording, or other, without written permission from the publisher.

First Edition
ISBN 978-0-9918437-2-5

acknowledgments

I wish to express my gratitude to all those who helped with
fundraising for this project:
Mike Pearson, Gillian Pearson, Cathy & Aaron Mathers,
Titania Michniewicz, Kimberly Scot, Sara Davis, Carole Summer,
Donna Nett, Rod Barcklay, Marg & Ken Pearson,
Vicki Nyari and David Hutter.

Thank you to Randy Morse for professional guidance and
Kevin Stanway for his talents editing and proof-reading.

Thank you to the crazy idea that set all this in motion,
to Collette and Kim for letting me stay in your beautiful
houses and feel like I was on a writing holiday,
and to Ben, Titania, Tira and Max
for encouragement when I needed it the most.

Tell a wise person, or else keep silent,
because the mass man will mock it right away.
I praise what is truly alive,
what longs to be burned to death.

In the calm water of the love-nights,
where you were begotten, where you have begotten,
a strange feeling comes over you,
when you see the silent candle burning.

Now you are no longer caught
in the obsession with darkness,
and a desire for higher love-making
sweeps you upward.

Distance does not make you falter.
Now, arriving in magic, flying,
and finally, insane for the light,
you are the butterfly and you are gone.

And so long as you haven't experienced
this: to die and so to grow,
you are only a troubled guest
on the dark earth.

Johann Wolfgang von Goethe

1...**the beginning**...1
all life is story unfolding

2...**opening ceremony**...3
a world of all possibility

3...**wherewithal**...8
attracting resources

4...**source**...17
you are a creative being

5...**offering**...25
living in an abundant universe

6...**expression**...33
rising to meet the challenges

7...**solidarity**...41
the voice of your heart

8...**unity**...55
being a magnificent part of the whole

9...**valour**...66
the confidence to rebuild

10...**harmony**...75
living in tune with instinct

11...**accompaniment**...84
the presence that is always with us

12...**celebration**...89
your true self is encouraged

13…**equilibrium**…98
the balance of heart and imagination

14…**envision**…107
broadening the scope of your dreams

15…**the void**…116
the point where there is nothing

16…**intermingle**…122
blending together for a rich life

17…**enticement**…127
well-disguised temptation

18…**obliteration**…133
having your socks knocked off

19…**wisdom**…138
nothing is beyond you

20…**inklings**…145
bringing ease and grace to life

21…**renewal**…151
making way for a new story

22…**astuteness**…159
a clear mind and discerning eye

23…**artiste**…164
dancing with joy

medicine bag…168
about the author…170

{1}
the beginning

Life isn't about finding yourself.
Life is about creating yourself.
George Bernard Shaw

You are a writer. Regardless of whether or not you have ever thought of yourself in this way, every time you put together a series of words, you are creating a story. All life is story unfolding. Are you happy with your tale?

If I told you right now that there is absolutely nothing that can't happen in your life, would you believe me? Can we even begin to fathom the idea of no limitations?

What most of us have forgotten is that we're not writers who work alone. We are actually part of a huge writing team that exists on many different levels. Think of yourself as the director. Your job is the big vision. There are writers who figure out the details that make things happen. They set up chance meetings and lucky breaks. They orchestrate life while you live it.

Your life is happening in real time. It isn't a book that's already written. The future is wide open with endless possibilities. For that matter, there's no reason the past can't be remembered differently, too. The more set in stone we consider life to be, the more set in stone it becomes.

Why live a life that is ordinary? You have the opportunity to make yourself into a legend. You can be a character that lives an epic tale. As you put together words to create action, growth, feelings, relationships, and magic, you begin the journey to find your inner hero. Your story builds as you meet challenges. Climaxes fill you with elation and denouements bring wisdom and understanding.

So let's begin a new way of looking at the world. Allow these words to move through you and unlock forgotten spaces. Be prepared to dream and to create. Open your heart to all possibility and enjoy the ride. Your unique and personal magnificence is waiting to be written.

{2} opening ceremony

Dreams are the seeds of change.
Nothing ever grows without a seed,
and nothing ever changes without a dream.
Debby Boone

In the beginning there was you—pure light and pure potential. You chose to incarnate into a body that came with a whole story of its own—physical weakness and strength, genetics, and imprinting from your mother's womb.

Next came the experiences of early childhood that shaped you. Experiences of love and joy gave you hope, experiences of pain and disappointment may have left you wondering about purpose and fairness. You were taught how to behave in certain situations. You learned how to protect yourself. Your mind is a computer that became programmed: if this happens, then do that. Sometimes, like the computer stalling, you don't know what to do next. But the universe has a funny way of revealing information and guiding us in subtle ways, especially when we need it the most.

We end up becoming our stories, even holding onto them when they cause us pain, because they are a part of who we are. Our stories give us structure. They give us a way to look forward and back and place ourselves in reality. Our stories create an identity for ourselves. In a world where people desperately want to fit in, we want our stories to be "normal". We hide away our tales that make us into something society doesn't want us to be—angry, hurtful, resentful, unforgiving… We tuck them deep into different parts of our bodies so we can forget that they're there. But they are there, they are a part of us, and they want to be known and acknowledged.

When we are born, we enter into a world of all possibility. But as we see the same things happen over and over again in our lives, it's easy to forget this. In order to be able to recreate our lives, we have to return to the belief that anything we imagine can be made real. We must return to the state of pure, heart bliss where there are no doubts or misgivings. Starting with a clean, fresh slate, we become inspired to dream our realities into being.

Everything you need to become what you want to be is already within you. More than learning how to do anything, we most often need to let go of the reasons why we believe that good things will never happen to us. Within the cells of our bodies are the memories that keep us locked into our predictable ways of thinking. Within the cells of our bodies is also the pure potential to make anything come true.

Perhaps one of the biggest fears we have is that if we let ourselves be pure, shining light, we won't be able to handle it. We purposefully keep ourselves down so that we can feel safe in mediocrity.

Every new journey begins with a first step. Finding the place inside of you where you can be without judgement is the first challenge. It is the place of the little child who really believes that magic is real. It is the place of the confident adult who knows that the world is her oyster. It is the place of the wise sage who knows that he has lived a life well spent.

When we let go of the idea of being a mere product of our stories, we energetically open up the range of ourselves. We become more in tune with our instincts, are guided by divine inspiration, and vibrate in communication with our higher selves.

Developing the power of your imagination is essential to being able to recreate your life. It has been your thoughts creating everything all along, anyways. Using your imagination to guide your thoughts in the direction you want to go is a continuation of what you have already been doing.

There is a trick to using your imagination to bring new experiences into your life. You have to imagine the details of a desired event but then let go of attachment to it happening exactly that way. You are trying to create the feeling of really being there and details are a tool for that. Imagining the details with all of your senses—what the food tastes like, what colors you are wearing, how warm the sun is on your bare shoulders—this is what allows you to create the feeling of satisfaction in your body. Once you have felt satisfaction, then you are able to recreate it with more ease every time you try. Eventually you aren't even trying any more because your life is just satisfying. The details of your visioning are a means to an end. If you let go of wanting life to unfold exactly how you've imagined it, you leave space for the universe to throw in some new twists that make it even better.

You can develop your imagination by practicing. Start by seeing yourself in a situation that you want to manifest. Really take the time to see what is around you and who else is there. Breathe in and experience how your body feels in this situation. Where is the tension? What are the feelings that are holding you back? When you start to identify the thoughts and feelings that keep you repeating the same patterns, you begin to draw a map of which beliefs you must let go of in order to be free and creative.

We need to start our new journeys as blank sheets of paper—pure and white, crisp and clean. Make a commitment to yourself to step through the door and cross the threshold into a new world where you are the master programmer—where you are the creative energy in charge. It takes a lot of listening to find the place of being a pure white sheet of paper. The voices in our heads that have been keeping us safe don't want to be erased. If we don't even listen to them, they won't be able to be released. Start your journey by really listening to each of the voices in your head. Accept that they are not your true voice. Start to identify whose voices they are and pinpoint when they came into your head in the first place. Listen closely and see how the voices make you feel in your body. Listen without judgement.

Hold the real you in your heart—the pure, white-light part of you. Hold the wisdom that you are already everything that you need to be. Separate this white-light part of you from the voices. Really integrate into yourself the knowledge that they are not the same thing. You are not the voices in your head.

You have started your journey. You have returned to your innocence. You have returned to your ultimate power. The voices will not go away so easily—they will demand that you listen to them. But now you know, in your breath and in your body, that you are so much more than that. You are pure, white light ready to embark on a new journey that will take you anywhere you can dream. You are inspiration welling up. You are intuition speaking clearly. You are the ultimate you, ready to become manifest.

I was in acting class at university in my early twenties. Our assignment was to keep track of the judgemental voices in our heads for three days. Every time we had a "you should" or "you shouldn't" or a "you're so…" kind of thought, we were to write down the thought and whose voice we thought it was. From the list itemizing who said what, we were to identify our top three judges. Naturally, my mother was one of them. Then in class, using my trained imagination, the exercise was to invite my imagined mother into the acting studio and perform my prepared monologue for her. We each had a partner in this exercise to witness and watch over our emotional well-being. I stood on the area designated "stage" and took a deep breath to prepare myself. I was amazed at how tense and emotional I felt. How difficult it was to open my mouth and speak, even though my mother wasn't actually there. As I continued on, it became easier and easier to shine without judgement. By the time I had finished my monologue, the thought of my mother watching me no longer made me especially nervous and tense. My body was free to perform. That was the day I experienced in my body that I was not those negative voices in my head. I was the person acting in front of the voices in my head. That is when I knew there was more to me than I had previously thought and it was going to take some great investigation and releasing to get to the bottom of who I truly am.

{3}
wherewithal

*Those who contemplate the beauty of the earth
find resources of strength that will endure
as long as life lasts.*

Rachel Carson

So what is a pure ball of light to do next? This beautiful planet Earth has been gifted to us as a place where we can come into the third dimension to live and laugh, to learn and play. Our pure light selves are seeds that germinate and grow into whatever wonderful people we choose to create. Coming into the third dimension allows us to interact with a physical universe, giving us the opportunity to see what is around us and choose our tools and resources.

Everything that you need to carry out your creative endeavours is available in this dimension. First off, you are given a body that moves in space and feels emotions. You are given the Earth itself, rich with abundance. You are given creative power and inspiration. You are given a mind that focuses your intentions and the power of love as the driving force of your actions.

When we recognize the endless abundance we are given, that abundance opens up and becomes available to us on many levels. When we are caught up in the voices in our heads, believing there is lack and we are undeserving, opportunities pass by unrecognized.

To harness our true creative powers we must embrace limitlessness. We must truly believe in our bodies, minds, and souls that there is nothing we cannot achieve. When we believe in ourselves and stop blocking ourselves along the way, the universe happily provides opportunities, connections, resources, and insights to guide us.

It is time to take stock of what is kept close to you in your life. What are you holding onto that it would be beneficial to release? What are the resources available to you that you're not using to their full potential? What brings you comfort and who supports your journey?

Take a look at what you support through your actions. Where do you spend your money? Is it in line with your beliefs, hopes, and dreams for this planet? Are you willing to release yourself from the conditioning of institutions and advertising in order to reawaken your inner self and fly free?

We can honour the Earth and show gratitude for all she gives by recognizing that each item we buy has a consciousness of its own. There are people who can hold a well-used object in their hand and tell you its history. Just because it's plastic doesn't mean it isn't a connected part of everything. When we buy things without care, or don't treat our possessions with respect, we jeopardize our relationships with the Earth. Our mindless consumption and disregard for garbage indicates our feelings of separation from the divine. Just as we need to be mindful in our thoughts and our relationships to keep them pure and strong, we must learn to be mindful with our possessions.

So much manufactured product is designed to be disposable; we have created a gap between ourselves and Mother Earth. We see her resources as something for us to use and pile up. We throw things back at her with no concern. This is not being a connected part of the life cycle. What if you tried for one day to live your life without creating any garbage? What if we actually took actions to replenish the Earth rather than mindlessly tossing garbage here and there? What if we used our imaginations to find new ways of using things instead of throwing them out, or if we found a new home for what we no longer need. Surely there is someone who could benefit.

Even if the things you own were made in a factory without any caring thought put into them, you can imbue them with consciousness through your relationship with them. You can give them life through your gratitude and respect. Treat your possessions as you would a person or animal and they will work harmoniously with you towards your goals. Better yet, when you are in the market to buy something new, if possible, seek out something that has been made with conscious intention. Give children handmade gifts that radiate the love of their creator. Talk to local crafts people to see if they can make what you have in mind. This way you will have a personal connection with the object, too. Go to farmer's markets and meet the people who are growing the food you eat.

Being free of attachment to the physical world doesn't mean you have to own nothing in life. It means you won't be devastated if you lose what you have. It means you aren't basing your personality on your possessions. It means that you are not in competition with anyone else to see who can own more.

Everything that happens in life is a tool that can help you create the life you want. Every word you speak leaves an energetic mark. Every purchase you make either benefits or takes away from the greater whole. Every action that you choose sets you closer to your higher purpose or leads you further down a road of distraction and disbelief.

Heading out on a new venture, it is important to take only what we really need. On a backpacking trip, it could be perilous to bring the kitchen sink! Simplicity is the clearest path in any direction, so it becomes necessary to take stock of what we already have and clear away what is not going to serve us on our journeys. It can be thrilling to discover that we already have much more than we originally thought.

Start with a list of what you think you need in your life, then look at the list a few more times to see if it's really true. Finally, release your attachment to the list and see what the universe has to say. Remember that whatever our plans are, they are not likely to unfold exactly as we envision. In fact, they're likely to happen in an even better way if we're willing to let go of our own ideas and follow the opportunities presented to us. After all, we are only human beings and our powers of imagination are just beginning to be cultivated.

It's important that we have a good base camp in place from which to explore these new ways of being. If you are not secure in your basic survival, that may be a good place to focus. As long as your body is not secure in having shelter, food, and warmth, your imagination will struggle to run wild. Again, it's time to look at the very basic needs of a human being. If you are putting all of your resources into keeping up with the Joneses—a fancy car, the latest appliances, fashionable clothes—then that is your choice, but it may distract you from achieving your true purpose.

Just as we must clear our minds of misguided voices, we must clear our lives of clutter. As our minds and environments become more clear, we are able to truly receive the abundant gifts of the universe. We are able to connect more deeply with our true selves and develop space in our lives to receive insightful guidance.

Explore what happens in your life when you begin to express yourself in new ways. What happens if you offer compassion instead of anger? Take the time to notice the gifts you receive in exchange. What happens if you don't buy something you have been conditioned to believe you "need"? Take the time to think about your purchases and how they will nourish you and the planet instead of being depleting.

Think of yourself as a vessel that contains all that you are. If you have filled yourself right up with beliefs and ideas, confident that you know exactly how it all is, there is no room left for change. If you want to change your story, you need to change some of your beliefs. In order to make room for new ideas and inspiration to emerge, you must create space.

Human beings tend to be very result driven. We want everything we do to have some effect. If we're making dinner, we want it to be appreciated. If we're doing someone a favour, we want to be able to call it back some day. What happens if we try doing something just for the sake of doing it? It may take some practice to let yourself truly play without expectations, but this is where creative genius reveals itself.

Play with what you have right now, instead of being focused on how to get what you need to do something else. You may find yourself pleasantly surprised that your present resources are beneficial in ways you hadn't dreamed of yet. Watch little children play. They can make anything into anything with their imaginations, even a stick or a stone. One child's creativity sparks another's until they are off on an adventure together purely for the sake of fun.

One of the greatest things we can do to move ourselves to a higher vibration is to recognize the gift in every experience. As long as we are critical and judgemental of our lives, we live in a place of dissatisfaction. We will not accept the possibility of abundance and joy. What an amazing feeling it is at the end of a long, hard day to look back and focus on the gifts and lessons learned. Even in trying times, there is always a positive thought you can come up with, even if it is just that you learned to never do that again!

Perhaps you will learn that you have more courage than you thought. Perhaps you will learn that if you stay in your heart centre, instead of engaging in a battle of wills with someone, anger and frustration actually dissipate. Perhaps you will recognize that changing one little thought has the power to completely alter the outcome of a series of events.

When we decide to acknowledge the little ways that things come to us in our lives, be it resources, companionship, or happiness, every day we strengthen our belief that magic truly happens and we are a part of it. No matter how big your grand vision is, the little things happening along the way make it real. Don't underestimate their power. Each new skill you acquire increases your abilities and each new thought is a milestone. If you need to see to believe, then start looking around you. You are manifesting results every day in every little way. Believe it!

When you separate yourself from the voices in your head that want to engage in a negative battle—they want you to feel useless, awful, and angry—everything is seen in a new way. You will see it from the part of yourself that is pure light. You will recognize the gifts that move you along on your way. Beautiful moments will abound and just what you need will drop right into your lap. This is your birthright.

Take moments throughout the day to recognize and appreciate all that is nourishing in your life. How many gifts did you receive today? There was the light that turned green just as you got there. There was the appreciative smile from a customer at work. There was simply the way the wind moved through the trees, creating a moment of pure beauty as you walked by. Our lives are full of gifts, so much so that we don't even stop to recognize or acknowledge most of them, but they are there and they are personally created for each one of us to help us on our way.

If you are feeling a lack of specific items in your life, try taking a journey in your imagination to see how it feels to have them. As long as you are stuck in a feeling of lack, you will continue to lack. Bring the feeling into your body of how excited and appreciative you will be to have what you desire. Believe that it has already happened. See all of the details of how it will look and feel. See who is there to celebrate the moment with you. Focus on your gratitude and gratitude is what you will attract.

You are a magical being of pure light that is constantly attracting exactly what you need in any given moment. Sometimes what we need is a challenge to awaken a new power in ourselves or a new way of thought.

Everything you need to make your dreams come true is at your fingertips.

If you make a list of what you truly believe you need in life to maintain your existence, then, once you have met those needs, you can let go of the word "need". Using the word "need" makes you needy. Being needy attracts more neediness. While there may be a part of you that feels unsatisfied, it is really a wonderful opportunity to feel comfortable with emptiness. Emptiness is where magic brews. It is the cup of potential to be filled. Instead of it being a space inside of you that identifies with lack and yearning, it can be a seed waiting patiently for the conditions to be right for germination. If it germinates too soon, it may be killed by a late frost. Cherish your empty spaces and wait with trust and anticipation for the time to be just right.

What goes on in your mind acts as a magnet to draw opportunities to you. Words alone will not change your life story, but they will attract new possibilities for action. While there is great benefit to visualizing your new life and putting words to the pictures that form in your mind, it is acting within your new framework that is growth. When your mind is in alignment with infinite oneness, you experience moments of tremendous clarity. You walk in your truth. You attract the abundance of the universe.

I sat in my apartment in downtown Vancouver. For the first time ever, I was living alone. I had just broken up with my boyfriend and he had moved out. Having just graduated from university, I had a short-term job, but really my life was feeling wide open and I wasn't sure where to begin. I'd been going to school for 18 years, having other people direct how I spent my time and where I focused my thoughts. I was feeling a little bit lost.

I picked up the tarot deck and guidebook my ex had given me. I had looked through it briefly, but not really opened it up, so I started at the beginning with the first of the major arcana. There it was—just what I needed—a road map to life. It contained a traveller's path to healing, contemplation, harmony, balance, and celebration. After that, every few months when I felt discontent, I would open my book to the next card of the major arcana. I was always gifted exactly the information I needed to move forward. It became one of my greatest resources and opened my eyes to the abundance of the universe.

{4}
source

If you would be a real seeker after truth,
it is necessary that at least once in your life
you doubt, as far as possible, all things.

Rene Descartes

Now you know that you are a being of pure light and pure potential. You recognize you are a physical body in the third dimension, a dimension full of resources to achieve your highest dreams. You move through time and space, recognizing that your thoughts create the reality that unfolds before your eyes.

It is time to take full responsibility for your life and its patterns. This is no easy task. Few want to admit, when things are difficult, that it is their own train of thought that led them to this place. We want to blame our circumstances on others, bad luck, or fate. When we are deep in a pit of despair, it can be difficult to believe there is hope for change, but there always is. Change begins by going deep inside of yourself and remembering the part of you that is pure light. Change comes in baby steps, finding something positive and nourishing everyday.

We are given many cultural concepts from the moment we are born that direct us how to live. There are many concepts we take for granted, not even considering whether or not they are true. It's time to start making lists and lists of everything you believe about every topic that matters in your life. What are your beliefs about marriage? Money? Relationships? Are those beliefs really serving you as a unique individual, or are they simply fitting you into a category? Are they holding you back or moving you forward? Get clear on which concepts are benefitting you and the greater whole and which are only benefitting a small part of one given society. Probe your mind with curiosity and dare to be different. There is absolutely no reason to believe what anyone else believes just because that's what everyone else believes—no reason whatsoever.

If it feels like you are struggling to swim upstream, you may have to dig deeper to discover what is impeding your progress. When things are difficult, it indicates another layer to be addressed. Really, there are four or five main beliefs that affect everything we do in our lives. Beliefs about not being good enough, not being deserving enough, or being abandoned and alone wreck havoc on just about everything we try. Everyone believes these things to varying degrees. Some people give the impression of being confident, but it is a front to cover up deep insecurities. Look at what's happening in your life for clues about your beliefs.

There is so much media trying to sway our beliefs about how we should look and act. Fear is perpetuated by telling us about every little scary thing that happens. Markets are controlled by telling us what we need to fit in. Our beliefs are influenced by guilt and shame. There is no reason to be influenced or directed by media. We may have the feeling that we will be out-of-touch with the world if we don't, but really we will be filtering out massive amounts of negative energy that bombard us every day. If something significant happens in the world, you will hear about it without reading newspapers or watching the news, especially if it is something that directly affects you.

Surround yourself with beauty and uplifting music, books, films, and people. Seek out media and entertainment that inspires and leaves you feeling good. If you want the overall "feeling good" factor in the world to go up, it will never happen as long as you're focused on things that make you feel bad. You are not deserting your fellow mankind by not keeping up with the suffering across the world. Instead of reading about it and feeling bad, do something about it if you are so moved. Instead of living in fear, surround yourself with light and create a life where you feel safe.

Seek out the patterns that repeat themselves in your life. As long as you are thinking in a similar pattern, the events of your life will continue to unfold in similar cycles. In order to change your life, you need to change your thoughts. Once you have identified a thought that is most likely holding you back, try thinking the opposite of it. If you have been thinking, "My boss is such a jerk," try thinking, "My boss is such an understanding guy."

It is the thoughts that go on in our minds while we are experiencing life that shape those experiences. Two people can be doing exactly the same thing and one will have a great time and the other will say it wasn't fun. Training ourselves to look for the positive will give us more positive experiences. Being open and accepting of how an experience unfolds, instead of going into it with preconceived notions, will put us into the flow of life where we can be greeted with lovely surprises. If we think we know what's going to happen, that's what will happen. If we are filled with wonder at all of the possibilities, we open the door for something new to come along.

You may feel like there is no way this world will ever be able to fulfill your dream because of its current state of being. That is quite possible. That is why you are a magician who is able to create a new world. You may wonder how a single person like you can change the world, but really you can. Every time you choose to think outside the box, you are creating a new pattern. Because we are all connected, everyone instantly becomes a part of the new pattern. We may not be conscious of it or act on it immediately, but it will be there. When you share your new idea with others, the momentum of it grows until it blossoms. That is why it is so important to hold onto your feelings of peace in times of despair, instead of losing hope. You are a part of the potential for change and the world can become a completely different place. We may need to be patient, but just by believing it's possible, it already exists.

If you think of life as an infinite series of parallel universes, then every time you have a thought, it instantly exists. Think "I'd like to play the piano" and somewhere in space and time, you are a piano player. Consciousness is not required to exist in a single universe. Having free will means that we are able to choose which stories we want to experience and go there. So, once you've imagined yourself playing the piano, it's simply a matter of acting in a way that will lead you to that universe where you play. It already exists. There is no reason to doubt that it can be.

Our doubts manifest as negative thoughts. We simply don't believe that what we want is possible and will come up with all of the reasons why. We get caught up in a cycle of negativity that breeds more negativity. What we really want is to feel the opposite way—to feel encouraged and excited about life. If thinking that life is boring is starting to bring you down, make yourself think the opposite of boring; life is fascinating and engaging.

Notice how it feels in your body when you think negative thoughts, then notice how it feels when you think positive thoughts, even if you don't really believe them for now. Which thought truly feels better in your body? Try saying the words out loud, focussing on them and their meaning. Why not choose the thought that relaxes your body and helps to make you feel better about life? Because really, everything is possible. There is no limit to what we can think. Ultimately, there is choice. Choose what feels best for you.

The beauty of thinking opposite thoughts is that when it's done with regularity, you will notice that reality begins to shift and change. You start to notice the ways that your boss is understanding. You start to receive the positive feedback you desire.

Look at your life as a practice field. If you were just starting to play soccer, would you expect to start scoring goals right away? You would start watching your teammates to see how they are playing and you would listen to your coach for feedback. Each time you play, you expect to be a little bit better. It's pretty hard to keep doing something in life and never get any better at it. There may be days when you're not really on your game, but practice does make perfect.

Every time you catch your mind being judgemental, critical, or caught up in worry, use a catch phrase of your choice to interrupt your train of thought. Your catch phrase might be, "Here I go again" or "Bla, bla, bla". Then immediately think the opposite of what you were thinking. Focus on it as long as you can. If you find your mind returning back to its original state, interrupt as needed. Just as children practice to tie their shoes, we need to practice control of our thoughts. It may feel like work at first and will require effort, but with time it happens more naturally and we actually catch ourselves experiencing spontaneous moments of joy. That sounds pretty good, doesn't it?

When questions arise in the process of exploring opposite thought, don't hesitate to test them out to see what rings true. If you have been believing that nobody likes you and you want to try believing you are well received, go out and act like they like you. Don't get all caught up in looking to them for proof, the test for truth is how it feels in your body. You must act as if you are truly liked, regardless of how the people around you react, and see how it makes you feel. Feel it to believe it. That is the point when magic happens and you change your story—the point when you truly believe.

It is time to create a new you—a you that is vibrant, confident, caring, and successful. Taking the time to think the opposite thoughts of what you have been thinking and really feel the difference in your body, not just in your mind, you will begin to actually recreate your cells. Imagine how it would feel to go through your day with everything unfolding with ease and grace. Imagine how relaxed and calm you would feel. Imagine how excited and appreciative you would be. Breathe these feelings into your body to cultivate them.

In order to get where we want to go, we have to have a general idea of where we want to be. Once we have imagined where we want to be, then it exists and we just have to get there. So, start trying the idea on. Instead of thinking "Why would I be the one to get the promotion?" try thinking "Why am I the one to get the promotion?" See the difference? The first sentence is infused with doubt and the second shows that you understand that on some level, it's already happened. We are asking ourselves "why?" all day long about endless things in our lives. Why this? Why that? Make your questions to yourself open doors instead of closing them. "Why am I so amazing?" "Why is my love helping to bring more joy to the world?"

Every moment of everyday is yours. You choose how you spend your time. Even if you feel like you have to go to the job you don't like so that you can afford to live somewhere with your children, the bottom line is that this is still your choice. You could choose to be homeless. You could choose to live somewhere else and do something else. Once we accept that we are actually in control of our lives and are not the victims of society, then time becomes our own again. Surely everyone can find at least five minutes to do something they love—something that makes them feel good.

We may be so caught up in our lives that we don't even remember what makes us feel good, but there is something for each and every one of us. We were all born with a unique set of talents and something beautiful we can do to share ourselves with the world. The key to reclaiming our power is to remember our talents and dedicate ourselves to them. Find something to be devoted to—be it a hobby, sport, or just enjoying hanging out with yourself—and make the time in your life to do it.

A friend of mine decided one summer to do something he called the Manifestation Project. He gave each participant a blank notebook to use for a month, filling it up with intentions for our lives and observations of how they played out. I started the month by jotting down a few vague things that I wanted, afraid to focus on anything too specific for fear of failure. Within the week I was recognizing that it was effective for me to write down some general intentions in the morning and then in the evening reflect back on the day and see how they had come about. I would write things like, "Today I intend lovely surprises" and at the end of the day I would see how many lovely surprises had come my way. There were always some. It made me recognize that we are all intending and manifesting every moment of every day, sometimes we just need to take a closer look to really see the connection. One day I was feeling particularly bold so I intended to find some money. Within a couple of hours I was doing the laundry and found a two dollar coin at the bottom of the washing machine. "OK," I thought, "that's a good start, but surely I can do better than that." That afternoon I had the unpleasant task of going through a big pile of old paperwork. I thought, "I'm just going to do a quick sorting and head outside." Well, during that quick sorting I happened upon an old government cheque that had somehow been forgotten. It was for $546. "Wow! This stuff really works. What a lovely surprise."

{5}
offering

My bounty is as boundless as the sea,
My love as deep; the more I give to thee,
The more I have, for both are infinite.
Shakespeare *(Romeo and Juliet)*

We limit ourselves by believing the voices in our heads saying we aren't good enough, there isn't enough of anything or nothing is ever going to get better. We see only what is in line with those beliefs. We experience only what fits into our current concepts of reality.

The truth, however, is that the Earth is endlessly bountiful. There is no limit to the abundance that is available for harvest. Everything is possible to the wild extremes of our imaginations.

It's unfortunate that we live in a world where the distribution of wealth is so unbalanced because the truth is that there is plenty for all. Our patterns of thinking come from generations who believed that life is a struggle and there is never enough. Those beliefs became the legacy many of us have inherited. It can be so challenging to really, truly believe that the Earth is endlessly abundant—that there is no reason we need ever experience lack. It is our expectations of lack that create lack. When we clear our minds with gratitude for what is, then we create abundance.

There has been much written these days about quantum physics and the idea that it is creative thought energy that directs the formation of what we call reality. When you close your eyes and clear your mind of thoughts, everything is possible. When you open your eyes and engage your thoughts, some things become more probable. It will never be the same for two people because we are each unique in our thoughts. Every occurrence in our lives gives us expectations of how reality will unfold. Will we see the cup as half empty or half full?

Nature has a different way of operating. It just is. When a seed lands on the forest floor, it doesn't think, "Oh, I don't have what it takes to become a tree. Good things never happen to me and there's no way this is going to work out." The seed knows that it is pure potential. It knows that with the right environment, it has the information needed to grow into a towering tree. It may even wait for years for the conditions to be right.

The seed quietly knows that when its potential is combined with the bounty of nature—the rich forest loam, the rain that falls, the sun that shines—then it will blossom with its true nature. The growth of the tree is fuelled by the love of the universe. It is supported in its growth and doesn't sabotage itself with doubt.

We, too, are little seeds of pure potential. We are imprinted with a pattern to flourish into amazing human beings. We fuel ourselves with the abundant resources of Mother Earth. We grow with the encouragement of clean water and are cared for by the sun. We only limit ourselves with the voices in our heads.

There are things we need to accomplish our goals. Mother Earth is the womb of creation that will bring forth the resources we require. If we have thoughts and emotions that need to be expressed, nature is our foundational support. The wind whispers in our ears, the sun fuels our passions, the water carries our intentions and the earth keeps us grounded and solid. By taking the time to observe nature and to connect with its magical properties, we give ourselves the confidence to believe that we, too, are part of nature.

We are not separate entities that live by a different set of laws. We are the same creative potential. We have access to the abundance and wisdom. We need only to feel and listen, to absorb the richness and simplicity of it all. When we feel that connection in our bodies, then we know that we have not been left alone to struggle. Nature has never abandoned us. Mother Earth has and always will care for us—her children.

There is no need to worry that our requirements will not be met. It is worry that brings about scarcity and fear. Things may not always happen the exact moment we want them to, or they may not unfold exactly the way we expect them to, but they will happen according to our intentions and beliefs. When we send out the energy of gratitude for all that is, reality responds by giving us more for which to be thankful.

Everything we have in life, including our bodies, is made from Mother Earth. There are many cases where we have taken her raw materials and altered them beyond recognition, but everything is still made from wood, metal, air, water, earth and fire. We feed ourselves from the earth, no matter how processed the food is. The Earth is our true mother, nurturing and supporting us.

When we appreciate that everything that has happened to us in our lives has been for a good reason, no matter how difficult or painful it was to experience, then we can recognize the gifts within the struggles. Our memories are just that – memories. They no longer have any connection to anything solid. You cannot go back and re-experience the exact time and place of the story. It is a moment that is gone.

You can, however, go back in your mind and recreate the story. There is no law that says we must hold onto our stories exactly as we've been remembering them. In the days of bards, before stories were written down and made stagnant, tales were alive. Each teller would add his or her own twist to make the story more exciting and entertaining. We have the power to do this same thing with our stories. There is only one thing telling us we must continue to remember an event the way we remember it—it is the voice telling us that we must continue to remember the event the way we remember it.

Be bold, be brave—choose to recreate your painful memories in a way that brings you joy and satisfaction. It takes a little bit of practice, but you can go back to your uncomfortable memories and rewrite the story the way you would have wanted it to work out. It takes focus of your imagination. It takes a true willingness to let go of the story you call your past. It takes a true desire to recreate your life. You can change the characters. You can change what was said. You can change it all. None of it is "real" in the way you have thought.

Our memories are like pathways. The more they are walked upon, the more established the trail. Once you have imagined a new creation of the memory in your mind—the one that brings you comfort and satisfaction—you must continue to walk the new path until it is well established. You must not let yourself be tempted to step back into the old memory. The more you use the new path, the quicker the old path will grow over and eventually be something that once was but is no more.

Recreating memories will have effects that ripple forward into your present life. The abundance of the universe will unfold before you, guiding you towards your true identity. The release of painful memories will actually change the physical make-up of your body and you will become a new and beautiful you. You will become a you that is supported and confident, a you that looks forward to an abundant future.

Have there been times in your life when something was being offered to you and you turned it down, then later regretted your decision? What is it that keeps us from receiving something being offered? Perhaps it's a voice telling us we aren't worthy. It's possible we're afraid of change or even afraid of feeling good. We may have been told something is bad for us or that good people don't do such things. The list goes on and on. Regardless, as long as we're denying ourselves abundance by being stuck in our minds, we're blocking what's trying to come our way.

When the universe is ready to hand us something wonderful, we need to have an understanding of the ways we sabotage ourselves. Perhaps we ruin things just so that we'll be able to say, "See, I told you nothing good ever happens to me." Be clear about your worthiness and allow yourself to feel good. Practice feeling good with little things so that when a big moment arrives you don't panic and fall back into your old patterns. Set out each day to experience fully all that life has to offer.

Accepting that we are an integral part of the universe, we also become a part of the source of everything. When we are the source, there is no longer any need to seek outside of ourselves for what we believe is missing in our lives. We are the source of energy exchange, so when we give, we receive. When we receive, we give. We are the source of love—by loving we are loved. By sparking our imaginations with the seeds of change, we are the source of manifestation.

We can instantly start receiving more from the universe by giving to ourselves. If you want to be a writer, give yourself an afternoon at a little café with your laptop. It doesn't even matter what you're writing about or if anyone will ever read it. You are giving yourself the experience. You are giving the universe your pleasure. Once it knows where your pleasure lies, it will bend over backwards to accommodate you. If you desire food in your belly, see if there is something you can do to help others have more food. Don't be afraid to give or you'll be trapping yourself into scarcity thinking. Maybe there's a soup kitchen you can help at or some way you can share what little you have with someone else in need. Trust that the universe will respond. Clear your belief that there will never be enough and allow the abundance of the universe to flow in your direction.

In the process of giving to others, we get a clearer picture of who we are. By paying attention to what we are drawn to give, we gain insight into our passions. By being strong for others in emotional times, we discover just how capable we are. As we bring gifts out from inside of us, long-lost aspects of ourselves are brought to the surface. We remember our true potential. Through giving we are blessed.

When I was a teenager, I was in a talent show at my school to celebrate graduation. I was a dancer and had the opportunity to do a solo of my own choreography. That was at the height of my dark days of depression and not understanding what my place was in the world. Dancing was the only thing that kept me alive. So, naturally, I chose a song that was a bit dark and melancholy—a song of lost love. It was a sombre piece, but I believed it had an inherent beauty of its own. The audience was thrilled after I performed and I had people I'd never met before approach me to share how much they had enjoyed my performance. But the two people that I really looked to for approval—my mom and dad—stayed silent the whole way home with no congratulations or appreciation.

I held this memory of their silence inside of me for many, many years. Always I walked the path of this memory with pain and disappointment. It affected every other time I performed. Finally I learned that I could recreate my memories, so I went deep into my imagination and relived the walk from the theatre to the car. I used my imagination to hear my parents speak all of the words that I was longing to hear. I saw us celebrating my performance together and felt their pride radiating towards me.

Not long after recreating this memory, I was talking to my mother on the phone about an upcoming opportunity I had to dance again. I walked down the path of my new memory in my mind as I awaited her response. It was so interesting. She started to say something that would have been typical of the old way, but only two or three words made it out of her mouth before she stopped cold. Then she said something encouraging instead.

JANET PEARSON

I was so astonished. I had actually recreated my life story and the ripple effect had recreated my mother's life story. There was such a feeling of peace and appreciation.

{6}
expression

Who then is free?
The wise man who can command himself.

Horace

Realizing that our physical realities are directly related to our thought patterns, it becomes time to take charge of ourselves and practice being in command. Life is pure potential and we are life. The universe is abundant and full of resources. When we recognize the patterns of thought and action that have been holding us back throughout our lives, we are one step closer to releasing those beliefs and learning to fly. The universe wants us to fly—it supports us in our dreams, completely. You need never worry about being good enough or deserving enough because in the realm of pure light, there is no right or wrong. There are no "shoulds".

Creating a new structure for your life that allows for your highest expression comes from the decisions that you make everyday. Every time you choose foods to eat, entertainment to watch, or people to associate with, you are choosing the structure of your life. Every moment that you spend working affects the overall theme of your existence. Every activity you choose for pleasure is a reflection of your inner being. Every time you spend money, you support the actions of other people in the world. Every conversation you have reflects your ability to trust and be compassionate.

Taking a close look at the actions of your life will help you to become more clear about the beliefs that guide your actions. So often, we become overwhelmed by daily life and let ourselves run on automatic pilot. It is easier to just pick up some take-out food and spend the evening being mindless in front of the television than it is to become conscious and take responsibility for our lives. But at the end of the day, how does that leave you feeling? Are you satisfied with your choices? Are you overflowing with joy and creative energy? Are you experiencing deep, fulfilling relationships?

Everyday life is full of effort and satisfaction. It's part of the continuous growth cycle. Think of what it must take for a seed to germinate under the ground and push its way through the earth to reach its first leaves up to the sky. It is the energy we put into effort that creates forward movement in our lives. Effort leads to accomplishment and accomplishment leads to satisfaction. Satisfaction inspires us to reach higher and takes us back to effort.

In order to replace the beliefs that have been running our lives for us, those values given to us by our early caregivers, teachers, and media experiences, we need to replace them with beliefs that nourish and inspire us to make the most of our lives. Identifying these beliefs (eg. I'll never have enough money), then finding the opposite thought (eg. I am in flow with the abundance of the universe), is the first step to taking command of our lives. Next, using one of the many forms of therapy available for altering beliefs (like Emotional Freedom Technique or Z-

Point), will actually change the subconscious decisions and actions we make in life. We can keep telling ourselves something over and over again, but until we start to really work with our subconscious programming, we may not notice results.

Try writing the new beliefs you want to embrace on little pieces of paper and put them up around your house as constant reminders. It took a lot of repetition to program your mind in the first place and it will take more repetition to reprogram it. The key is to stop using the old pathways. The more you divert your thoughts to the new path, the sooner the old ones will grow over and you won't even remember where they used to be.

Weed out all of the beliefs that are working against you. Take a good look at what you believe about money, careers, relationships, and health. Are these beliefs a hindrance or are they in line with the highest truth?

This is your part of the co-creative process—this, and getting out and doing things that move you closer to your goal. Obviously if you want to win the lottery you need to buy a ticket, but what else can you do to participate in your grander vision? Perhaps you can start researching organizations with which you'd like to share your millions. You could find ways to start giving of yourself or the resources you already have. You could draw up a business plan or look into investment possibilities. Act like you already have all the money you desire. See how it feels to be this new you by creating consistency between your thoughts and your outward actions.

Maybe you have talents that have been forgotten in your life because of the advice of others. Perhaps you were told in grade five that you couldn't sing, so please stop trying. Possibly you wanted to become an artist when you were a teenager but the lure of a good-paying job drew you away from your passion. The universe embedded you with talents to lead a full, rich life—a life that adds to the overall positive vibrations of the world.

Try to pull lost talents out of the closet to engage with them again. Does it reawaken parts of you that feel like they have been missing in action for years? Starting to paint again may rekindle the thought patterns that you really are talented and worthwhile. Pulling your bike out of the garage to go for a ride on a sunny day may help to revive your sense of joy that will then overflow into your relationship with your kids. Anything can happen. Open the door to see what flows through.

Everyone is good at something. Even the person who believes they have nothing to offer, has some area of talent. They may not recognize it, but it is there. There may be things that are a natural calling for us but we've ignored them because someone, at some point in our lives, told us we couldn't do it well. Someone else telling you that you lack talent does not make it true.

Probably the easiest way to identify your talents is to think about what you really like to do. Brainstorm this without the limitation of how you can make money—this is about finding your true identity, not about finding a job. There may be things that you've only dreamed of doing but have never had the opportunity. Still, in your heart, you know that it would be right up your alley. Dream big and then, dream bigger.

Regardless of what the rest of your life looks like, find some way to incorporate a little part of what you like to do into your daily life. You may have to be creative about what this looks like if you have expensive interests, but there must be something you can do to move in the direction you want to go. Once you are truly in sync with your given talents, opportunities will magically arise out of nowhere. Figure out how your talents can help to benefit the world, in ways big or small, and you will be supported in your endeavours. This is your opportunity to give of yourself in a unique and beautiful way. Even if doing something just gives you a little more spring in your step, you are doing the world a great service. Don't underestimate the power of simply being you.

Time and money are two of the greatest resources that we are given in this life. Unfortunately, they also tend to be the two things we believe will always be short of supply. But, the more consciously we use the time and money we have, the more we are in their flow and the more they will continue to flow in our direction. Always spending your time doing things for others, without taking care of your own needs, may leave you feeling exhausted and bitter. Guilt may keep you from doing something beautiful for yourself. It's a trap—a continuous cycle. As long as you don't take care of yourself, you are never properly taking care of others and time will always seem insufficient.

The same thing happens with money. When we aren't caring for ourselves properly, we tend to spend more money on just getting through the day—multiple coffees, food that drains our energy even more, or gadgets that promise us a better life. Money is an energy force that is meant to flow, but if you are always giving your money to people who are depleting the earth, then the direction of flow is towards depletion.

If you spend your money consciously, really understanding that you are affecting the entire world with every purchase you make, then you are choosing the direction of the flow. Some days this may not be easy, as the right choice is not always the easy choice or the obvious choice, but it is an investment in the future for many generations to come.

It is time to become clear on your goals so that you can hone the skills you need to achieve them. State your intentions clearly to the universe and it will support you in making your dreams come true. Take command of your beliefs and actions. Rid yourself of the woe-is-me attitude and walk forth bravely as the warrior you are, knowing that every apparent set-back or challenge is an opportunity and gift in the greater plan of your life.

We can choose to view our efforts as struggles, feeling like everything is working against us and it is always a battle, or we can choose to take our lives as a challenge. Deciding that we have what it takes to meet any challenge the universe gives us, we are in a position to celebrate each step of the way. We already know that we will be successful as each moment we move closer to our ultimate goals. What may have been seen as set-backs are viewed as time for reflection and regrouping. Obstacles give us the opportunity to be still and really listen to intuition.

If we wait around for the universe to give us all that we hope for, we may be waiting for a long time. Don't forget that as a co-creator, you play an integral part in the process. It probably won't be very effective to wake up and intend to win a million dollars that day, even if in your heart you really, really want to win a million dollars. Not that it isn't possible for you to win big money, but first you have to deal with the beliefs you have that stop you from winning.

Intend that today you will believe the universe is abundant—that it's possible for money to grow on trees. Believe in magic. Believe that good things can and will happen to you. Intend to be completely grateful for all that you have, knowing that you are a wonderful, deserving human being. Intend to deepen your connection with the natural world so that you are more present in the flow of giving and receiving. Intend to use all that you receive for the highest good of all.

I went to university and ended up with a Bachelor of General Studies with a concentration in English and Theatre. My plan was to be a high school drama teacher. My junior high drama teacher had suggested it to my Mom once during a parent/teacher interview. After getting my Bachelor's, I needed to do one more year to get my teaching certificate. It was a program that required an application and acceptance. So I applied and waited to hear if I was accepted. In the meanwhile, I did some volunteer work at a local high school with the drama department. The teacher there was very well respected and when we were done our time she told me that she didn't really recommend that I become a drama teacher. "Sports get all of the money and support," she said. So off I went with confusion in my mind. I remember standing out in the woods one day with all of these voices ringing in my head—being a teacher's a good job, you would make a great teacher, you don't want to be a teacher… I had to look deep inside of myself to realize that I didn't really want to be a teacher and work within the public school system. When I received the letter saying that I wasn't accepted for the program, I wasn't disappointed. When I received a phone call a few weeks later saying that I was on the waiting list and there was room for me if I wanted it, I took a deep breath and said "No, thank you," with confidence. I found my way down to my own voice—the voice of my truth. I went on to become a teacher in many different ways, but not within the public school system.

{7} solidarity

> *To enjoy good health, to bring true happiness to one's family,*
> *to bring peace to all, one must first discipline and control one's own mind.*
> *If a man can control his mind he can find the way to Enlightenment,*
> *and all wisdom and virtue will naturally come to him.*
>
> Buddha

Once we begin to hear the true voice within our thoughts, the next challenge is to make that voice a comfortable part of ourselves. It is one thing to repeat affirmations while you're brushing your teeth, and it is another thing to have positive words of joy just flow freely from within to be shared with the outer world. It can be a great leap to move from having a new way of thinking within to actually communicating and interacting with others from a new heart-felt place, mainly because we will continue to be triggered into our old ways of reacting.

There is a part of you that has become what it is in order to keep you safe and protected in your lifetime. Every method of reacting that is a part of your character has arisen from a real need. This personality you have developed seems to be as much a part of you as the part that is pure light. It can seem like your best friend and worst enemy at the same time. Retreating into your conditioned ways can bring comfort and security in trying times. It may be that this part of you doesn't want to be changed. There will no doubt be some resistance.

It is possible to remain friends with these conditioned parts of ourselves and still reduce the amount of control they have in our lives. There is darkness contained within the light. It's the yin yang—the Tao. When we try to deny the parts of ourselves that we want to change, in a way we only end up making them stronger. Denying the darkness in ourselves also gives us fuel to judge. When we embrace all parts of ourselves, we become more compassionate to the struggles of others.

Often the voices in our heads that give us grief are really just looking for sympathy. The voice of anger is looking for understanding and the part of us that feels wounded is looking for compassion. We can try to receive sympathy and understanding from the people in our lives—our lovers, friends, and family—but undoubtedly, it will never be satisfactory. What we really need is to awaken our own abilities to be sympathetic, understanding, and compassionate towards all of the parts of ourselves.

There is a lovely visualization that can be done to find a new home for wounded parts of yourself, rather than trying to drive them away or deny them. If you take the time to really connect with that part of you – the part of you that is lonely, for example—and make an effort to like that part of you, you will become more whole with all of the parts of yourself, those you consider dark and those you consider light. Create the lonely you in your mind's eye. See what he/she looks like and take the time to listen to what he/she has to say. Treat this part of you as a little child that you wouldn't dream of judging or chastising. Remember that there is a friendship between your higher self and this part of you that wants to be released from its stagnation.

Then, in your mind's eye, find a new home for this part of you. Imagine a beautiful place where the lonely part of you will receive what he/she needs to be fulfilled. Thank this child-like part of you for all of the gifts and protection he/she has provided over the years and then see him/her running free, basking in a new, peaceful home. Know that just as this part of you has taken care of you in so many ways, you are now able to take care of it. There is no more denial. There is no need for banishment. There is acceptance and gratitude.

By coming to peace with the parts of ourselves that have tended to cause conflict in our lives—the parts that led us to saying the wrong thing at the wrong time—we will find that our interactions with the world begin to shift and come from a more balanced place. When the cries for help and attention that come from the denied places of ourselves are calmed, our true voices can be heard. When our true voices are heard, we begin to recognize all of the opportunities the universe is giving us to flourish.

There is a part of you that the world is waiting to receive, this light from within that will shine so bright it will inspire and bring joy to all of those around you. Perhaps you haven't been so well received in the past. Perhaps you have felt misunderstood and judged. It is not uncommon, then, to want to withdraw and give up. But you must believe that the world is a better place because you are in it. You must recognize that you have a unique and personal contribution to make to the world.

By getting past the voices that are telling us what we "should" do, and by finding our inner places of balance where we don't react out of anger and fear, we are able to communicate and interact so much more effectively. We are able to get down to the real matters at hand. By becoming friends with the dark parts of our own personalities, compassion is awakened for those same places in others. By letting go of the conflict within ourselves, we are able to make the changes needed to lessen our conflicts with others.

When we begin to find the place where we can silently be with all the parts of ourselves, then we are able to be in a comfortable place of silence with the world. We will no longer feel like we always need to be trying to fix everyone around us. We will recognize that instead of needing to push other people's buttons in the ways we always have, we are able to give the parts of ourselves that we know will be appreciated and cherished. The voice that comes from within you will be the voice of your heart.

It can be helpful as you're trying to figure out what you believe and what is your personal truth, to take the time to express your thoughts outwardly, either by writing them down or sharing them with a trusted friend. Having to say things out loud often makes their true weight felt much more than just letting them ramble around inside your head. Discrepancies come to light and you feel how your words make your body react.

As you start to become aware of your thoughts and consciously look at them, it can also be helpful to stop talking so much. Instead of saying what you are thinking out loud in a reactive way to what you are hearing, try listening to what is being said and just ruminating on it. Observe your thoughts and look for the truth in them before sharing them with the world. When you are alone try expressing your thoughts out loud so that you can see how they resonate in your body and the air around you. Is this really what you believe and want to say? Write the words down and see how they look on the page. Is there another way you could express the same idea with positive, nurturing language?

Once you have found your way to express what you are feeling inside, find others that you can share it with—those whom you know in your heart will really hear and appreciate your words. Teach what you know by living it, listen to the feedback and be prepared to refine your thinking even further. Teach generosity by being generous and gratitude by being grateful. If you present your ideas with an open, loving heart, you will be well received and given new insight.

When we are able to express ourselves using "I" statements instead of telling others what we think about them and what they should do, it is much easier for us to express our true feelings. By saying, "I feel like this when that happens…" as opposed to "You always do this…", the tone of blame is lessened and others may be more receptive to hearing what we are saying. Also, when we are truly listening with our hearts, we are able to hear what others say without taking it personally. We can recognize that they are speaking from their minds with their own conditioning striking out. It is not the true feelings of their higher self. Be calm and be gentle. Don't let other's doubt work its way back into you. You may feel like you are all alone in your new way of thinking, but there are others out there who will be happy to encourage and inspire you. Be receptive to meeting them and they will show up.

If we are in the company of people who are being critical or complaining about the world, we can help to shift their energy by pointing out what is good and beautiful. We don't need to do it in a way that makes them feel wrong, but we are able to say, "I really like that person because..." There is always something positive we can say about every situation. We may need to dig really deep sometimes to find it, but it is there. Be a messenger of light. Even if the other person doesn't acknowledge what you say, they will have heard it on some level.

By having the courage to express our higher selves to others, we may inspire them to reconnect with their own higher selves. We can encourage this by letting them know how much we admire them and by listening to what they are saying. We can share the resources we have discovered along the way and the words of wisdom that speak to us.

With life being a reflection of our inner states of mind, it follows that the more you abuse yourself the more you will be abused. If you want to change the story of people always taking advantage of you, you need to start being respectful to yourself. As it is, so many of us say things to ourselves that we would never say to anyone else. We can be our own worst enemies. Every time we tell ourselves that we deserve what we're getting in life, we are paving the way for that treatment to continue. Every little abuse that we tolerate allows for bigger ones to take place.

The path away from being abused by others starts with you finding the voice in your head that is going to stand up for you. Once you are standing up for yourself, other people will materialize in your life to offer their support and understanding as well. You will have to be diligent. If you can't stop thinking the way you always have while you are in the company of the people taking advantage of you, do whatever it takes to get out of their company. Know that you are a divine being who deserves to be treated with the utmost respect. Respect yourself. Love the part of you that is suffering and find your voice to speak your truth.

It's really very sad how much energy we put into harming ourselves. Why is it that we have such low self-worth that we think it's okay to keep putting ourselves down and treating our bodies with such disregard? Even if we can't be motivated to stop hurting ourselves for our own sakes, perhaps we can find the impetus with the realization that when we harm ourselves, we are also harming the whole. There is nothing you can do to yourself without it affecting all of life on this planet in some small but not insignificant way. If not for you, find a way to treat yourself with kindness for the sake of everyone else.

Because it can be so difficult to try and change your thought patterns while you are still surrounded by annoying co-workers and whining children, you may need to find some space for yourself in life where you can be alone to reflect, even if it's just for five minutes that you lock yourself in the bathroom. When you feel like all of your buttons are being pushed and the negative voices are desperately trying to keep their hold on you, that is the time to get away.

It can be really helpful to have a practice to follow at these times. Start by acknowledging the part of you that is vying for control. *I love the part of me that is a loser.* Really focus on finding that feeling of love rather than trying to banish the thoughts of self-doubt. Focussing on love will bring you into your heart and connect you with divine light. It can also be helpful to have an affirmation to repeat. Even if you don't believe the words yet, the rhythm of repetition will help to calm you and it will give your mind something to focus on other than putting yourself down.

Take these little time-outs whenever you need them and eventually you'll find yourself doing it while you're still engaged with the people around you. They may be talking the same old stuff to you, but you won't be hearing it the same way. It won't trigger the same reactions and you'll be inspired to share a new perspective that will alter everything around you.

As you become more successful in your life, you may find that your appearance and outer ways need to change to reflect your growth. You may be associating with a different group of people who inspire you to put more care and attention into your appearance. Your desire to be able to inspire others may leave you wanting to present yourself in a more professional way. Your newfound wealth may give you the opportunity to purchase items of a higher quality than you were used to before.

It can be a little bit worrisome how your old friends are going to react to your new image. Many times we actually hold ourselves back, unconsciously, from being successful because we are concerned that our friends will be jealous and we won't fit in anymore. But really, all of this, like anything, is perfectly within our control. Whatever we believe, is what will happen. If we share our successes with our dearest friends, everyone will be uplifted. If we don't participate in outright extravagance and flaunt ourselves around town, we will be honoured with people's respect and admiration. As long as the new you is in line with your belief that you are a fabulous, deserving person, and not just a cover-up for feelings of insecurity, you will be remarkable.

If you think about how many mirrors there are in the world now compared to a few hundred years ago, you can understand how so many of us have come to associate our worth with what we look like, but we will never see ourselves as others see us. We will only ever see a two-dimensional reflection and more often than not, that reflection will have a critical look about it.

When was the last time you looked in the mirror and really looked into your own eyes? When was the last time you stopped at the bathroom sink and saw a person that you love looking back at you? Mirrors are an opportunity for you to see your own beauty, but you have to be able to see past what you look like. When you tell yourself that you're beautiful, then your beauty will radiate for everyone to see. When you can look yourself in the eye, then you will know who you truly are.

Perhaps you're feeling a little nervous about going out into the world and spreading your love. Perhaps you fear rejection. Unfortunately, it is our own lack of self-confidence that draws dismissal to us. Our love may be rejected just to help remind us that giving is not dependent on receiving. It is not necessary for our love to be well-received for us to feel the joy of expressing our highest selves by giving it. We must let go of expected returns.

Perhaps your love is not well-received because your need for approval has made the presentation too uncomfortable for the other person. You have come on too strong. Then the lesson is to refine the presentation with care to the other person's needs. We have to let go of our own motives and pay attention to others.

If you want to get past the feeling of always being rejected, find someone who really needs some love in their life. There are plenty of people who would be happy to receive your kindness. Learn what it feels like to be accepted and be grateful.

It is natural to receive some opposition from the people you know and love as you embark on this journey to recreate your story. They may be afraid that they won't be a part of your new story. They may feel like you are now judging them and their ways as wrong. They may scrutinize you and be critical of the new ideas you are trying to express. It will take courage for you to know when to hold your ideas inside of yourself and when to share them with others.

If you try to base your actions and reactions on what you think other people are thinking, then it is difficult for interactions to be based on any kind of truth. The truth is that you don't know what anyone else is thinking about you. Even if they try to express it, there aren't many of us who are really able to put the entirety of a feeling into words. Great poets have done a remarkable job throughout the ages, but even their work is always open to interpretation.

If you think that someone is angry with you, then everything they say to you will be heard through a filter of anger. It won't matter what they are really saying, because you will have already decided that they are angry. What you hear from them will actually provide evidence that they are angry because that is what you want to hear. None of it will be based on truth. We have to learn to listen without expectation colouring what we're hearing; only then will we be able to truly communicate with others and experience true relationship.

Each and every one of us is an artist in the way we combine words to create thought. We may not believe we are creative, but we are creating every moment of every day. We are creating every exchange that happens between ourselves and others, ourselves and animals, ourselves and life. By choosing to put particular words together in thought or to say them out loud, we are unleashing massive creative potential.

A painter who continually paints the same picture may be good at what he does, but may not be growing as a human being. A person who always responds to a situation with the same words may handle the situation, but she is only utilizing a small amount of her potential. When we are wishing that somehow things would unfold differently, we need to look at the thoughts we are having and the words we are using, to catch a glimpse of how things could be different. If we wait for some force outside of ourselves to come along and make a repeating pattern have a different outcome, we will be waiting for a long time.

As long as the painter uses the same brush strokes and colors, he will paint the same picture. Try mixing your words around to see how the outcome is affected. Instead of saying, "You never take out the trash" try switching it up to "I sure appreciate it when the trash is taken out". Subtle difference, but the energy of the statement is completely changed and it will move you out of a stagnant, repeating cycle into a whole new story.

Words have tremendous power over everything in existence. The words that go on inside your head are shaping you everyday. The words we share with others can inspire or crush. They don't even have to be said out loud to have a result. When we have a limited vocabulary, we have a limited effect in changing ourselves and the world. Seek out new words to use that have a blessing quality about them. Create a flower garden in your mind of beautiful images and choose new words to describe your inner life. Try thinking of the crumbling cement wall as determined rather than ugly and crappy. The people walking down the street are unique and interesting, not pathetic. Your new boss is inspiring you to find your inner confidence as opposed to being a real jerk. It may feel cheesy at first to think and speak this way, but the more you do it the more natural it becomes. Eventually, you will be conversing with other people who use the same language as you—happy, confident people who are not embarrassed to recognize the divine beauty in all life.

We are all looking for evidence to support our stories as we move through our lives. Magically, that evidence will always exist because our external worlds are a reflection of our inner dialogues. If your story is that he is mean to you, then you will keep experiencing moments that support your story. You expect it to be and it is. We may feel that we have no power to change anyone else, and in a way that is true, but we do have the power to change how we perceive others. If you change your story to one where he is kind to you, you will start to notice evidence to support that story. He may not be acting any differently at all, but you will be regarding him differently, which will change your experience of life.

Whatever it is that you are creating in your day to day life, be it preparing a meal, reading a story to a child, or manufacturing car parts, treat what you are giving as a gift. Select it with care and thought to who you are giving it to. Infuse it with feelings of love and appreciation. Tie it up with a bow of celebration to make everyday seem magical. Love has the ability to infuse all things. You are a channel for love. Channel beauty and light into everything you do.

As you become more and more talented in your chosen areas of life, you will begin to feel the effects of having some mastery. People will be appreciating your contribution. While you may have mastery of the physical process of what you do, there is always room to refine your presentation to the world. Now you are an instrument of expression and your trade is a tool. Are you sharing the message that you believe others want to hear, or are you sharing what is in your heart? Are you cutting corners to be more profitable, or are you creating with integrity? Your body is the channel through which your higher self is expressed. When the two are in tune, you flow freely within the creative energy of the universe; there is no limit.

When you become convinced of your own beauty, that beauty becomes a part of everything you do. You won't be able to walk down the street without others noticing your shining light. The brighter you allow yourself to glow, the more healing the world will experience. Don't hide yourself away. Recognize that expressing your inner light and feelings of joy will make everyone happier in the long run. There may be people who begrudge you your pleasure because they are lacking in their own lives, but on some level you will spark something that leads them towards remembering their own light.

JANET PEARSON

I sent a letter to my Dad once that I really regretted. It was to him and my Mom both, actually, but I know it hit him, and what I didn't know was that he was already down with a bad case of shingles. He didn't talk to me for some time after that. When I phoned and my Mom asked if he wanted to talk to me, he said, "I have nothing to say to her." Yup. When I wrote that letter, I was listening to all of the voices of should. I was angry at what I perceived to be an injustice. But I was too naïve to see that my perception wasn't the only one possible—that we live in a beautiful world of all possibilities, and no one is better than another. I got lucky. My Dad and I love each other, and the next time we saw each other in person it felt like the air was cleared with just a hug.

{8}
unity

*There comes a time in the seeker's life
when he discovers that he is at once the lover and the beloved.*
Sri Chinmoy

Beyond the voices in our heads there are also archetypal traits—honesty, confidence, compassion, etc. Every human being is a unique combination of every trait we can be. (High in confidence but lack honesty. Honest as the day is long but a little bit of a doormat. And so on.) Consider these traits all located somewhere within the yin yang symbol and you have male and female, dark and light.

We all have a light side and we all have a dark side. We all have a male side and we all have a female side. When there is true union between the male and female within, then there is ecstasy. Being a whole human being is being a united front made of the male and female aspects within yourself. When your inner world is in balance, your outer world will be, too.

So many of our stories are to do with discontent between the sexes. How many girls have stories of being terrorized by boys and how many boys have stories of girls being mean and nasty? We are pitted against each other right from the start.

But what is really going on is a battle within ourselves, trying to get clear on what is "good" and what is "bad". Where do we fall on the scale? Some want to be good. Some want to be bad. We become polarized within ourselves, but we are all the parts—the good and the bad. We are everything. We are part of that "one". Everything we witness outside of ourselves is sourced from within ourselves. If we see someone being mean, it is because there is a part of us that is mean. The key is to recognize that it is only *a part* that is mean. There is also a part that is kind. You may have not experienced one part or the other for some time, but that doesn't mean it isn't there.

As you develop a new trait in yourself, you will begin to see it more and more in other people. Where beforehand you may have looked upon them with judgement because you felt yourself lacking, you may now find yourself looking at them with admiration. Seek out opportunities to be around people with the traits you admire. Welcome these traits into your own being while clearing the thoughts that have been limiting you.

If there is a part of you that makes you feel uncomfortable, think about what that part needs. Usually when we're acting out it's because we're looking for some attention. *I love the part of me that is mean.*

What happens if we give ourselves the attention we crave? If we try loving all the parts of ourselves, then we'll know how to love those same parts in other people. What does it feel like to go beyond the division of good and bad into a whole you that is comfortable in your own skin, relaxed and breathing, knowing you are perfect?

How you feel on the inside will reflect on your outside experiences. You will start to notice things in a different way. How could you not?

Set an intention to notice beauty, even in the darkest places. Decide to love all of the parts of yourself. Go and talk to the part of you that is scared and reassure yourself. *I love the part of me that is scared.* Go to the part of you that feels abandoned and tell yourself that you're loved. Honour the parts of yourself that have been hidden away because you were told that girls don't behave like that, or boys shouldn't do such things.

It seems one of the best things we can do for the world is to be our whole selves. Imagine if we weren't motivated by guilt or how we "should" be acting. With unity comes a deepened connection to natural instincts. You will find yourself inspired. Break down all of the barriers you have put up within yourself and allow your spirit free range.

When you have found the part of you that is loving, then you will be loved. When you allow yourself to receive love, to really breathe it into your body, your very cells will begin to shift. Don't wait to find the right person that is finally going to love you the way you've always wanted to be loved. Find the person inside of yourself who is capable of loving you the way you've always wanted to be loved. What is within is without.

Let love lead you to meet your true self. Walk hand in hand with the most annoying parts of yourself and find compassion. Know—truly know—that no part of you is not good enough to be loved. Remember about being pure, white light? Don't forget that. Let your light shine within yourself. Eventually you'll be walking with a you whose company you really care for and enjoy.

One of the best ways to get clear on what we want in a life companion is to look at our past relationships to get clear about what we don't want. Then we familiarize ourselves with the opposite. So often we don't know what we want because we've never experienced it. It's time to become a researcher for this new story you are writing and seek out inspiration. If you know that you don't want to be with someone who is lazy, but you don't really know anyone who is motivated, you may have your work cut out for you. Of course, the first step is to love the part of yourself that is lazy and then cultivate the part of yourself that is motivated.

We are naturally attracted to people who have a similar vibration to ourselves. At first, it may seem wonderful, but after some time we realize that the same aspects that attracted us in the first place are now driving us crazy. This is the universe's way of compelling us towards growth. If, as a couple, we choose to address our limiting thoughts together, there is greater potential for deeper awareness and closer relationship. As long as we ignore the desire for wholeness, we will most likely continue to be frustrated with our companions. We will live in the delusion that it is only the other person, not ourselves, who needs to change. But as we seek out the higher truth for ourselves, it will be reflected in our relationships. If what we want is someone who understands us and sees us for who we are, then we must understand ourselves and celebrate our true selves.

As your thoughts become more positive and encouraging, you may find yourself attracted to new and different people. Remember that not every person that you are attracted to is destined to become a future lover. It is your similar creative energies that make you notice each other in the first place and it may just be that you have some wisdom to share with each other. It may last a moment or a month. It may just be the exchange of a smile. As you become more joyful, you will naturally attract the attention of other joyful people. Go with the flow and enjoy the pleasure of good companionship. Test the waters to see if there is something deeper that reveals itself, be it a mentoring relationship, business partnership or romantic coupling. Be open to change and change will happen.

Finding balance in a partnership is like playing the game where you put your hands together, choose a leader and mirror the other person's movements. After a while you switch who is leading. At some point you lose track of who's leading and realize that you're both moving together, sensing each other's impulses and desires. With two hearts open to each other, two hearts that are practiced at giving and receiving, communication happens naturally. When you are both fulfilled within yourselves, then there is no tug-of-war of wants and needs. You offer a helping hand just for the sake of it and know that when you hold each other, you are drawing from a common well of love.

When you and your partner are both clear about what it is you love to do, you are able to encourage each other's strengths and find ways to share your life without an imbalance of power. You may discover new skills you didn't know you had that allow you to share the work. You may find yourself willing to do things you don't really want to do just because it is a gift to your partner. When our areas of expertise are supported and honoured, we are willing to do things that bring us less enjoyment because we don't feel like the time we have for our passions is threatened.

As long as we can't appreciate our past relationships, we will be plagued with blame and bitterness. How can we expect to move into a new, loving relationship when we are still approaching it with fear and trepidation? Fear will be reflected back to us by a partner who is also afraid and untrusting. We must make peace with the past before we can truly move forward into something new. Otherwise, we'll continue to repeat the same scenarios over and over again.

Take a look at your past relationships and see if you can identify your repeating patterns. Perhaps your partners have all been really bad with money or unable to communicate effectively. These patterns are your patterns and they hold the clues to the beliefs you have that keep you in the same kind of relationships over and over. Clear the patterns of belief and you will be able to walk into something that offers new levels of insight and new opportunities for gratitude.

If you have inner conflict, there will be conflict in your world. If you are at peace, there will be peace. Considering that we all live on this planet Earth, we all have the power to be a part of creating real peace. We may get distracted and think that the work of peacekeeping is outside of us, by protesting, petitioning, or even fighting, but this is not the truth.

The only path to true peace is to stop being in conflict with ourselves. When we truly love all the parts of ourselves—even those that would be considered dark or bad, by judgemental standards—then there is no conflict. We don't need to fight to get rid of the parts which cause us shame. We need to love it all. Love is transformative and will take everything we experience out of being right or wrong. We are perfect in every moment. The opposite of conflict is acceptance. Accept your perfection and continue to grow into a person that it is comfortable to be.

How can we expect to be in a loving relationship with someone when we don't even treat ourselves with love? What do we know of love? When we are forgiving with ourselves, others feel safe with us. When we are giving to ourselves, others enjoy sharing themselves with us. When we treat ourselves with tenderness, others are drawn to compassion. We must first find the lover within ourselves and cultivate that relationship, then we are able to bring that relationship into the world.

You are a giver of love. The love energy of the entire universe flows equally through you as it does everything else. You may not feel like you can love because of fear or mistrust. Past relationships may have left you feeling bitter or disillusioned, but you are still love energy and you always will be. Forgive yourself for holding onto negative feelings about past relationships. Convince yourself that it is safe for you to love and reopen the door to your heart.

Practice in situations that don't require a huge commitment. Love the food you are eating. Love the neighbour's dog. Actually feel the love flowing out of your body without impediment. Life is so full of opportunities for us to express love and it feel so good to do so.

By reflecting on your life and finding the moments when you truly felt love, appreciation, kindness, etc., you can create a memory box that will allow you to open yourself even deeper to receiving. When you are feeling like your heart wants to close down, you can find a quiet place to be with those memories. They will rejuvenate your belief that it is all possible. However small the moments of joy in your life have been, you can feed their energy with your appreciation. You will cultivate joy, water it and let the sun shine down on it, and you will have more joy. The natural cycle of life will take care of that.

If we feel like we are doing all of the loving and not getting much in return, then we are misunderstanding the source of replenishment. The supply of love is inside of ourselves, not outside. As we cultivate our connections with Mother Earth and Father Sky, we open the inner channel for love to flow into us in the form of pure, white light. With so much love flowing in, we can't help but share some of it around. The beauty is that we don't have to share it with the hope of getting something in return because we are the source of our own replenishment. We are able to give without expectation.

Once you are open to giving love, the next step is to be open to receiving love. It is in this exchange between humans that magic happens. Kindness grows and joy is shared. Through the practice of giving to yourself, you must receive. Acknowledge any resistance and love it. It does not make us weak to receive—it does not mean we are needy. It takes great dignity to be able to receive gifts with appreciation. Once you appreciate your own company—actually enjoy being with yourself—then you will be open to appreciating all of the gifts that the universe wants to shower upon you. None of them will pass by unnoticed and you will be allowing others to experience the joy of giving. It's a two way street. Giving and receiving are two parts of the same experience.

Think about what you desire in a good friendship. Are you giving those things to yourself? Do you really listen to what you're saying? Do you compliment yourself when you look good? Do you enjoy laughing with yourself? Be your own best friend first and all of your relationships will benefit. Your friends want to see you happy and self-assured. They want you to be fulfilled in every way. Oblige them by allowing yourself to be content.

As much as it may feel like it sometimes, you are never without love. Your whole body can be tingling with love in a moment, if you let it. You don't need another person in your life to experience bliss. Stand alone in a field and let yourself be bombarded with ecstasy from all sides. Let it penetrate you from within and without. Experience that joy and you will have found a great source of personal power. You will no longer be a victim who is without. You will be a creator with so much love flowing through you that you can't help but share it with others.

Your true love partner is not any person living on this planet, it is you. It is divine spirit. You are everything and everything is you. Allow yourself to be swept away in this love that comes from all things. Offer yourself in union to all that is and take pleasure in the greatness of your being.

Truly riding the wave of love means experiencing it on a much deeper level than what happens in most human relationships. Riding that wave with another person may be your ultimate goal but you have to learn how to ride that wave alone first, by connecting with your divinity. Then, when you come together with someone, nothing impedes the flow of giving and receiving. Together, you find yourselves exploring the realms of divine love.

You may have noticed that there are some people in your life that are much more than just good friends; you feel you know them on a deeper level. In them, you see the face of the divine. You are always grateful for their presence in your life and never feel the need to criticize them. You accept them on their path and offer your love and support.

If you don't have people like this in your life, cultivate this kind of relationship with yourself first, and you will find them. The universe offers us all kinds of supporting friends when we are open to receiving them. The more we appreciate ourselves and others, the more appreciation we will feel.

Every person is a part of divinity. When you allow yourself to open up and really love them, you acknowledge that divinity and let the relationship take you deeper into your own source. Your understanding of the give and take of life grows through your relationships with others and your own divinity is revealed.

Relationships weren't working out so well for me. The past two had left me feeling disillusioned that I would ever find anyone who would accept me for who I am and not drive me crazy. In the meantime, I couldn't even begin to accept myself for who I was and I was driving myself crazy with all of the endless criticism and doubt in my internal dialogue. I participated in the World Tapping Summit one year and spent two weeks doing at least two hours of EFT Tapping every day. I tapped on my passions, abundance, physical health, the law of attraction, and personal peace. I tapped and tapped and tapped. A new voice began to emerge in my head—a voice that liked me and had confidence. I began to love the dark parts of myself that I hadn't even wanted to admit existed. With all of this clearing of old patterns, I began to feel more and more light. I started to get really clear about what I wanted in a relationship and what I wanted my next lover to be like. I took the time to make lists about all of my old relationships—what worked and what didn't—until I could imagine myself receiving the affection I desired. One day when I was standing in my garden, feeling how I had found this loving person inside of myself, I made the intention to bring the lover out of me and into reality. Not two months later, I met the most amazing man. He seemed to be all of the things that I was dreaming into being. Just meeting him was the inspiration I needed to know that a satisfying partnership could exist for me. I needed to find the lover inside of me, first; then magic took over.

{9} valour

*What we need to do to allow magic to get hold of us
is to banish doubts from our minds.
Once doubts are banished
anything is possible.*
Don Juan Matus

Power builds as we replace old, patterned thoughts with new, nourishing ways of thinking. Confidence grows as we experience ourselves for what we truly are. We walk taller and find it easier to speak our truths. As the conditioned voices in our heads have less and less significance, we catch ourselves smiling more often.

Now is the time to use this knowledge and confidence to rebuild the structure of your daily existence. Foundations will be built to support you in ways you never dreamed possible. Knowing that you are a perfect, creative, dynamic being, allows you to go forth bravely, trusting your dreams to unfold in their own way.

Pay attention to the things in your life that are working. The more you focus on the positive, the more positive energy will come your way. There is nothing like the feeling of gratitude—deep, heart-felt gratitude. It brings us into our bodies. It fills our hearts with light and connects us to all of the subtle energies that surround us.

One thing that keeps us from being all we can be is self-doubt. We doubt that we are deserving enough. We doubt that we have what it takes. We doubt that we are rich enough, good-looking enough, or smart enough. But our higher selves know the truth. They know the amazing skills and talents we have been given. Our higher selves know our secret dreams and won't let those dreams die.

When we strengthen the voice of our true selves within the conversations that run on and on inside our heads, we become more confident that the true path is to follow our dreams. It is the only path that will bring us the ultimate satisfaction we so desperately crave.

By looking at your successes, you may also notice gaps in your life. How have you given your power away? Are you able to look after yourself at a basic level? Confidence comes when you rise each day with the belief that you have what it takes to make your own way. What are your expectations for yourself? Your expectations—not others. Try making a list of your minimum life expectations. What kind of food do you look forward to eating? What kind of job is necessary to keep you satisfied? Are your relationships meeting all of your needs?

With a clear vision of where you already are and where you want to go, the path between the two becomes more obvious and instinct works to guide you. You will find your vehicle for forward movement along the road of success.

When we think about our greatest fears, so often our self-doubts are at the base of them. We don't believe we have what it takes to face whatever we are afraid of and survive. It is the fear of the unknown, not of anything real. We can spend our whole lives fearing things that never actually happen. What a waste of life force energy that is. We fear what might happen and by fixating our thoughts on that fear, we actually draw that energy towards ourselves.

Know that you are divine light and that you can face anything that comes your way. You can face it because it is you and you are it. Make a point of trying things you are afraid of, just to show yourself how truly great you are. With the confidence you gain, you will free yourself from being caught in an endless cycle of worry. This is the only moment that exists. Don't draw things toward yourself that aren't in line with your life vision. Be disciplined in your mind and use the tools you have to remain centered and certain.

When you take the time to celebrate the successes in your life, you create fertile ground for more of the same to follow. You build the confidence that success is your birthright. Self-doubt fades away as you cherish your accomplishments.

Once you have an idea of how you'd like your life to look, it's time to start gathering as much information and resources as possible to move in that direction. At first it may feel like you are taking baby steps, but as you gain strength and confidence, soon you will be running in the direction you want to go. You may even have to slow down because you're overwhelmed by how quickly everything is falling into place! If the choices you make move you in the direction of your dream, then you can't help but get closer to it. Surround yourself with inspiration—seek out items that will help you and stories of people who have gone where you want to go. If you are a painter, buy the brush that will help create your masterpiece. If you work with children, study new methods of communication to deepen your experience with them. If you dream of getting to outer space, cover your walls with pictures and imagine how great it will feel to be there. Watch movies, talk to people, do anything you can to move yourself in the direction you want to go.

Opening ourselves to allow spirit to flow through us, both by keeping our thoughts positive and learning to be in our bodies, we find ourselves having new desires and passions. Places we never dared go become enticing. We naturally seek out beauty and can appreciate it on a whole new level. Our creative juices flow and we are more confident that our sexuality is part of that same life force. We seek deep fulfillment, where once there was deadened acceptance. Our stories change as our excitement builds. We are daring truth seekers, driven by spirit, on the road to mastery.

As we wander through our days, we notice the things that make us feel good and give them more weight than the things that bring us down. As we deepen our connections with all life, we experience that just being alive feels good and that being allied with harmony for all life feels even better. Walk in the direction of whatever makes you feel good. Follow the call of your higher self.

It's strange how discipline and willpower become these out-of-reach concepts that we believe we should have, but don't. We figure we must either be disciplined or give up completely, forgetting the middle ground. But discipline and willpower are attributes to be cultivated and in order to clean up our minds and bodies to become true manifesting powers, cultivate them we must.

It's easy to stay who you are right now, even if your life is really difficult. There is no change required. There are no fears to face and you don't run the risk of disappointing yourself. Isn't that what we're good at? We set a new intention for ourselves and the moment we fall off the wagon, we give up completely and go back to the status quo.

The negative voices in your head are not going to go away the first time you ask them. These voices hold tremendous energy. That energy must be freed so it can be transformed. That means we must be diligent warriors. We must find our willpower when we're dieting to keep from having that chocolate doughnut, even though we know it would be immensely enjoyable. We must use willpower because chocolate doughnuts no longer fit into the grander vision of having a healthy body and feeling good about ourselves. Similarly, we must cultivate mental discipline to not participate in gossip or judgement. It may feel good in the moment, especially when everyone else is doing it, but it will never take you to the higher realm where your enjoyment comes from cheering others on from your heart.

Doubts may arise as you set new goals for yourself. It is a continual process of clearing limiting thoughts and refining your dream. You may discover another level of fear within yourself and have some more clearing to do before new insights will come. It's amazing, though, how when you truly begin to let go of your doubts, thoughts will pop into your mind seemingly out of nowhere. It's like one of those children's puzzles where the red triangle goes through the triangle spot, the blue circle goes through the circle spot and eventually all of the coloured pieces are inside of a ball. If your doubt is blocking the triangular entrance, then the red piece can't go in, no matter what. But as soon as the entrance is clear, you are that much closer to being complete.

There will be entrances and colours you didn't even know were there until some of the lower ones are complete. Some days it may feel like all the work you've done to change yourself has been for naught, but this isn't true. Most of our fears are buried because we haven't wanted to address them, but the only way for them to come out to the light of day is for something to happen that triggers us to experience them. As your relationship with your true self becomes more solid, these deeper fears naturally seek acknowledgement.

When you find yourself getting caught up in doubt and fear, that is the time to take action. You must shift the energy. Go for a run, yell into your pillow or just jump up and down. Don't try to shove the feelings back down—they will just come back up again with a vengeance.

Love the part of you that is scared because, really, that is all it wants. Laugh out loud and enjoy your fear knowing that it is not in control of you. There will be new moments of joy to follow, new heights to reach and new reasons to celebrate. Your higher self will not let you become stagnant in the moments of accomplishment and joy. It will take your confidence as a cue that you are ready to dig deeper. Accept this challenge with courage.

Once we hear the voices in our heads that love and support us, we are much more likely to be daring. This is what we need—to dare to dream, to dare to go where we never have before, to dare to make changes. With the understanding that there are no problems and nothing is ever failure, we have nothing to lose. It becomes hard to come up with a good reason why we shouldn't try something new. Those eager for an exciting story filled with adventure will welcome challenges, especially as the outcomes become more and more fulfilling. Even if it's just little adventures each day, we approach them with the courage of warriors because we are connected with the master teacher that lives inside of us.

Sometimes things may happen that seem like a set-back to you, or they won't happen fast enough and you will begin to get impatient. But as we are only a small part of a much grander story, there are always forces at work beyond our recognition. Patience can be one of the most difficult virtues to cultivate, especially when we are waiting for something exciting to happen. Just watch any small child who is waiting to go to a party. How many times will they say, "Can we go yet?"

By recognizing that for every event that happens in our lives, there are countless other events that must happen first to take us to that exact moment, we put ourselves into the universal flow. With trust, we are able to make decisions based on our instincts, which will put us in the right place at the right time. Cleaning up the chatter in our heads, we are able to vibrate at just the right frequency to attract positive experiences into our lives, experiences that are celebrated as successes. Then we know we are on the right path, even if strange things happen that seem contradictory to where we want to go.

There is a blessing in every mishap, even if we can't identify it. Sometimes it isn't until much later that we are able to look back and see how everything that happened was a perfect part of the story. By seeing mishaps in a positive light, we don't give in to self-doubt. We are able to maintain the confidence that all is good. The world does work in mysterious ways—become a part of the mystery.

Lots of times when we are trying something we haven't done before, we want to be able to do it privately or just in the company of people we trust won't laugh at us. But even if we are alone, if we allow the critical voices in our heads to participate, we aren't really alone. The real trick is to be able to do things like no one is watching, not even those voices. There is only your higher self finding a new way of expression. Your higher self has no need to be perfect on the first try. It revels in the idea that mistakes lead to growth. Your higher self doesn't use the word "wrong", so next time you're trying something new, invite it along to be your cheering squad.

Repatterning your belief system is not something that happens magically overnight. There may be some beliefs you are able to release as soon as you recognize them, but there are layers upon layers and some won't even be visible until others are altered. It will take determination, diligence, and discipline. You must be a warrior in training and keep getting back up to fight the good fight.

Some days it may feel that being committed to following a path that serves the highest good is restricting. You have chosen to eat pristine food but that makes going out for dinner a challenge. You have chosen to give a certain amount of your earnings to charity but that means you're on a tight budget this month. Know that every decision you make to follow a certain path will take you away from other paths but it will also take you to a place that only that path goes. The choice is always yours. Your commitment to a certain way will bring you freedoms you don't yet understand. It will take you to new places that will open up your life in an amazing way.

Several years ago I broke my shoulder very badly in a housekeeping accident (don't ask!). Living in a rural area, the hospital service was rather lacking. They weren't able to do any x-rays where I lived, so I had to drive almost 2 hours to a hospital where they could do them. I sat in agony all night and then the next day my brother drove me to the hospital. When I got there I was supposed to get two different x-rays, a normal one and a special one. They told me they only do the special ones on Thursdays and it was Tuesday. I asked if I should have the normal one done anyway and they said not to bother.

I went home and sat in agony for another two days and then was driven back again. As soon as the girl took the normal x-ray she said, "Oh, no!" It turned out that not only was my shoulder dislocated, but a chunk of the ball of the humerus had come off in the process. Within five hours I was in surgery. Afterwards the nurses all commented on how nice the incision was and told me that my surgeon had been the "shoulder expert". For several years I told this story as a complaint of how pathetic the hospital system had been and how it had failed me. I was bitter.

Then one day as I was telling the story again I said, "What happens if you're the guy who doesn't get the shoulder expert?" Suddenly it dawned on me how for years I had been criticizing the universe for a perfectly executed plan. Of course I had got the shoulder expert but only because of the x-ray mix up and having to come back again on Thursday. If I'd had the x-ray on Tuesday I wouldn't have had the shoulder expert and may not have regained the excellent use of my shoulder. Hindsight – it's 20/20. Now my story is about how great it was that I couldn't get an x-ray until Thursday!

{10}
harmony

The words of kindness are more
healing to a drooping heart than balm or honey.
Sarah Fielding

A beautiful thing happens when we open the door to new ways of thinking—our very body begins to realign itself and a deep healing takes place. We find the strength that comes with being in control of our thoughts and our lives and we experience the harmony of living in tune with nature and our instincts.

As long as we are using life force for complaining, we are constantly draining ourselves and bringing down the vibration around us. When we love ourselves and our lives, we bring joy and healing to those around us. Having a mind that is in alignment with your heart creates a beautiful balance that works towards the highest good of all.

What are the things that you are doing in your life that nourish you? When your heart says, "Take a nice, long bath" does your mind say, "Don't forget to do the dishes and take out the trash"? Believing that your heart knows what it is talking about, and honouring that, will change your life in so many astonishing ways.

Much of the stress we experience is caused by feeling like victims. We feel hopeless and out of control. We can't control the people around us. We can't control the economics of our countries. Many days it feels like we can't even control our own thoughts. Taking personal responsibility for our lives—really accepting that what is happening on the outside is a reflection of what's happening on the inside—is scary. It means we have to admit things we don't want to admit. It's much easier to blame hard luck on outside forces. It can be easier to believe that obstacles are insurmountable, so we might as well just give up trying. We can escape into television, become workaholics, or indulge in food and drugs. We can convince ourselves that all our problems come from the world around us.

As long as we remain victims of existence, not much is going to change. Opportunities will continue to pass by and our experiences will be less than satisfying. But with the knowledge we have gained so far, it is no longer desirable to stay in that victim role. Knowing that we are pure light—pure potential—and that we have the resources and support to achieve our dreams, our souls yearn to go further. Knowing that our inner dialogues are reflected in our outer experiences, and that we have the power to be in command of our experience, takes us to a place of inner harmony. We have the confidence to speak our truths in a way that supports all life. We are not victims. We are creators.

We are not victims of the diseases that affect our bodies any more than we are victims of our life experiences. We have the power to heal ourselves through our confidence and diligence. The choices we make every day continue to affect us for years to come. Cleanse your body and mind to see how the synchronicities and coincidences in your life begin to line up and move you towards your highest dreams.

Becoming aware of your wholeness and unity with all life, leads to new strength within yourself. Where there used to be confusion that would lead to anger, there will be understanding and insight. Where there used to be judgement and dislike, there will be forgiveness and appreciation. You will move away from being a victim of your story—outraged that so-and-so did this to you—to having a heart that is full of understanding and compassion in the face of so-called atrocities. Your body will be so happy that you are cultivating this strength because with it comes deeper breath and a more relaxed nervous system. Your emotional system will be delighted to have the freedom to experience joy and your spiritual being will finally have the relationship with you that it has longed to recover.

Perhaps all of your dreams have been squashed by fear. Nelson Mandela suggests that it is the fear of how powerful we truly are that keeps us from being great, not our fear of failure. We might fear we won't be able to maintain our visions once we get there. Maybe we're concerned that if our lives change too much, we'll lose our friends, family, and social structure.

Just as we are afraid to let go of our limiting beliefs, those that have guided and kept us feeling safe for so long, we fear walking into higher states of being because it is the unknown. Our doubts have protected us. What will keep us safe when we're living the dream?

Luckily, the heart is ready to step in and take on this role. The heart gets so ecstatic when you are in your groove that it pumps out feelings of knowing it's all good. The adrenaline rush that comes with experiencing your true creative power will keep you wanting more.

Your body knows exactly what it needs to be healthy at all times. The trick is to get past the voice of superficial desire to hear the voice of instinct. Another trick is to move beyond the products that are offered to us everyday, those with all kinds of claims. Then we can be clear about what is nourishing us and what is not.

Other than our original eight cells, the cells in our bodies go through a complete cycle of replacement every seven years. So, if you set your intention to become a more vibrant, healthy you and hold onto that, in seven years every cell will have been recreated with that intention. You literally will be a whole new person.

Our bodies are made up of what we feed ourselves, the air we breathe and the water we drink. That is what we are. The higher the vibration of the food we eat, the higher our own vibrations will be. It's that simple. If you are polluting your body with low vibration foods, ones that are deep fried or full of chemicals, then it will continue to be difficult for you to hear the voice of your true self.

Healing your body comes with taking the attitude that you deserve the very best. Healing comes through cleansing. All of the things we consume that our bodies don't know what to do with get stored away here and there—in an organ or a joint. Eventually, this stagnant energy causes more severe problems. Just as we need to cleanse our minds of thoughts that sabotage us, we need to cleanse our bodies of deposits that keep our energy levels down. As our bodies begin to vibrate at a higher frequency, so will our minds, and when we are vibrating at a higher frequency, that has a positive effect on everyone else around us.

If you choose to eat cleaner, healthier food, then your body will become a better conductor of spiritual energy. Just as water flows more freely through clean pipes, your clean body will offer less resistance. People doing juice fasts often report amazing abilities to manifest almost instantaneously. A body bogged down by digestion, especially the digestion of so many ingredients that it doesn't even recognize, is just that—bogged down. In order to clearly transmit our intentions to the universe, we must see our bodies as a spiritual tool that needs to be maintained in excellent working condition.

You don't need anyone else to heal your life. But you do need to be in touch with your true self to heal. As long as your decisions are based on information pumped into your head by institutions and advertising, or even well-meaning relations, you won't be following your true path towards healing. Everyone's path is different. What is curative for one may cause problems for another. Clearing yourself of energetic ties to your past and learning to breathe in the sweetness of each and every moment, will leave you knowing in your heart what is right for you. When you honour yourself by seeking out the very best food available and giving yourself the space and time in life to pursue your dreams, then you have become your own best healer.

While we tend to believe that we live in a solid, physical world, it is actually made up mostly of water. Water flows. It affects our emotions and carries our prayers. You are water, the air is water and matter is water. That means there really is no division between you and everything else. If you want to send some thoughts of love to someone far away, there is a free flowing stream directly between you and them for your intention to float upon. Tell your wishes to the water and it will hear them.

A great way to deepen your connection with water is to take a trip to visit your watershed. No matter how far away its source is, your water is coming from somewhere other than pipes and taps. There is a point where it is falling rain and melting snow and it runs freely down a mountain side. There is a river that carries it to your town. Follow the river until you find the place where you can sit and appreciate the beauty of its movement. When you turn on your tap back home, you will know the source of that water. You can imagine it in its glory and infuse it once more with sparkling joy.

Water has the ability to dissolve things that are hard, crusty and caked on. Given enough time to soak, it will break down impediments and clear the way for life to flow. Do you take the time to appreciate the water in your life? Is the purpose of your morning shower just to get clean or do you allow the water to wash your emotions and spirit as well? Let yourself flow with the water and ask it to help wash away all the aspects of your being that no longer serve you. When you drink water, intend for it to cleanse your body and bring new life force to all of your cells.

If you think about the expression "frozen with fear", then it makes sense that during life experiences there are parts of our bodies that are frozen. Little bits of you, here and there, have closed themselves off in hopes of not being pushed too far. Eventually, you may find it difficult to feel much of anything. Your body wants to be free flowing with the waters of existence—it wants your breath to reach every cell, bringing nourishment and inspiration.

Try taking some time to just lay still and check in with your body. Try to put your consciousness into your hands. Imagine energy running up and down each finger and up into your wrists. If you get to a place where your imagination doesn't want to go, that's the place to direct your breath. Breathe into that spot and imagine there is an ice cube that is thawing. Send your love to that part of your body. If a memory arises, love it. If it causes you pain to think about it, use your imagination to recreate it into a memory that makes you feel satisfied to release the energy that has been held there for so long.

Having some form of physical activity in your life will do wonders to help clear away what has accumulated in your body. Your body wants to sweat. It wants your heart beat to go up and push fresh blood and oxygen to all of your cells. Physical activity cultivates determination and discipline. It takes you out of your mind and into your body and allows you to act in a more instinctual way.

We make ourselves more dense than we're meant to be by holding onto fear, guilt, and shame. When we clear the baggage of the past, it feels like the wind can blow right through us, the sun can shine right into our bones, and the wisdom of our ancestors can play with our souls.

The parts of you that feel hurt are the parts that want loving the most. Doesn't every child who falls from his or her bike really just want a hug and a band aid? They don't want to be lectured about how they were riding too fast or weren't paying attention to where they were going. They don't want to be told that they were stupid. They don't want you to blame their friend for their fall. They just want to know that they're still loved.

When something happens to you that feels like your heart is breaking, let the love flood in. Think about anything that connects you to love. Don't fall into blaming the world for what happened or you'll just cultivate bitterness. No band aid can make that feel better. Let love be your band aid.

Once you've found some things in life to help keep you grounded and centered, add them to your medicine bag. If you find ways to enhance your intuition or you find words that inspire you, keep them handy for when times are difficult. These are your tools; they are the tricks of your new trade.

In your role as co-creator, you are a channel that generates ideas and sends the energy out to the universe to make it so. Mother Earth's energy comes into you from below and Father Sky's energy comes into you from above. They meet in your heart with your wonderful new idea and your joy explodes the creative force out to all realms. The cleaner and healthier your body, the more you feel this channel open and flow with energy. Use your imagination to strengthen this flow. Take time every day to see the Earth's energy flowing up from the center of the planet, through your feet and up to your heart. Imagine all of the power of the sun, moon and stars directed down through the top of your head and meeting and mingling with the Earth's energy in your heart. The clearer this channel, the more powerful your intentions. The more powerful your intentions are, the stronger your creative ability will be.

I was taking a class through the local college, to learn how to make herbal remedies at home. The teacher introduced us to using a pendulum to figure out dosages and product suitability. A pendulum is just as it sounds. It is a weight (maybe wood or a crystal) hanging from a cord that swings freely. We were taught that when you ask the pendulum a yes or no question, it will swing in a circle in one direction to give a 'yes' answer and in the other direction to give a 'no' answer. I picked up the pendulum and instantly had great success with it swinging answers to my questions. The universe knows all; every answer is just waiting in the ether to be accessed. The pendulum became a dear friend to me and I use it in many aspects of my life to know what will benefit me and what will not. Years later, I moved on to muscle testing, using my fingers when I didn't have a pendulum handy. Muscle testing has given me a direct route to my inner knowledge. I use it for deciding what foods to eat, how to plant my garden, what kind of supplements will benefit me and even whether I ought to take the right road or the left. As my vibration becomes higher, my muscle testing is more accurate. The more I muscle test, the less I need to because the answers just appear in my mind as intuition. I know what is best for me and having that confidence helps me to shine my light on all those around me as well.

{11}
accompaniment

We have all a better guide in ourselves,
if we would attend to it,
than any other person can be.
Jane Austen

Deep within our hearts there is a presence that has been with us since the beginning, a presence that knows no boundaries. As children, we were much more inclined to flow with this presence. We connected to it by joy, a sense of awe, and wonder with the world. We heard its voice speak to us of life's amazing potential. Its voice guided us when we had decisions to make. Mostly we weren't even conscious of this voice, we just felt that we were wise.

As the years went by and our doubts began to grow, the sound of the voice was muffled by disillusionment. New voices entered that demanded attention and insisted on being followed. Decisions that once flowed with the nature of all things became difficult. They became motivated by guilt and apprehension.

But this presence has always remained within us. It is eternal, loving, and wants us to experience true potential. It is the part of us that always has been and always will be. It is the ultimate teacher that can guide us so effectively in our decisions because it has access to all of the information that we, in our limited scope of being three dimensional beings, can't always retrieve.

When you quiet the "should" voices in your head, the ones that think they know what is best for you, then this true guiding voice will happily be there to whisper bits of inspiration into your mind. As your confidence grows and your days are filled with more and more moments of pure joy, you will walk your path knowing that you are not alone to figure it all out yourself. The universe wants you to be successful even more than you know.

This presence guides you to hold your own in difficult situations, keeping a warm feeling in your heart so you don't spiral off into the chaos of your mind. It guides you to cross the street and enter into an old bookshop, leading you to exactly what you need in that moment. This guide encourages you to approach the person that inspires you and strike up a conversation.

Sometimes, you will feel this guide as intuitively knowing the answer to your questions. Other times, when you are challenged with weeding through the voices, taking the time to relax and breathe, formulate your question with clarity, and seek the place within you that is without judgement or expectation, will help you find your answer. Sometimes the answer will appear outside of you—a particular word in a poem that helps life make sense or something a stranger or movie character says that rings clear and true.

When you ask, the answer will come. When you reach out to connect with forces beyond yourself, you step into a new flow. It is only our beliefs that we are all alone in the world that keeps us from developing these deeper relationships. It is a relationship that is worthy of cultivation because your guide is your biggest fan. This guide will help you harness courage and belief in your own innate wisdom. It is your astute friend that never has selfish motives, will always be available, and believes in you without fail. The answers you receive may push you beyond some of your known boundaries but they will always be in your best interest when you ask from your heart.

Dealing with what we once saw as failures becomes easier when we remember we are not alone in making things happen in our lives. If we don't get the promotion we were counting on, we are able to understand that it is because something better is coming our way. Instead of falling back into old thought patterns of how we never get what we want and nothing is ever going to change, we are able to move forward with trust that there is grand scheming going on in the higher realms and we are in line for something beyond our wildest dreams.

The presence of the guide is nourishing. When it is strong, you will feel like you are floating in a sea of comfort and bliss. You will feel your body as calm and relaxed. That is how you know you are connected; it feels good. When we make decisions with our minds that go against what's best for the greater good of all, we know it in our bodies. We try to ignore the fact that our breathing is shallow and there is a real tightness in our stomachs. We try to write off how horrible it feels because the voices in our heads have convinced us that we are acting as expected. However, succumbing to the expectations of society is often not the path that leads us to success. We need the courage to break free from all of those beliefs and do what feels right for us. Do whatever feels right in your body. Do whatever brings you that feeling of self-assurance and peace.

Don't be afraid to use your imagination to cultivate your relationship with your guiding presence. Give your guide form in your mind's eye. Give your guide a name and seek out where he or she lives. Treat this relationship as you would any other, by cultivating friendship, having a laugh, and sharing gifts with one another. Recreating the story of your life begins in your imagination. It is the greatest tool you have to initiate change.

Walk your path with the knowledge that your guiding presence is always with you and when you are unsure which way to go, the answer will appear. You will feel confident that the words you speak reflect your inner truth and you will experience yourself as you are truly meant to be—boundless and free.

In my early twenties I was attending the Stein Valley Voice for the Wilderness Music Festival. There was a strong First Nations presence there, many of them dancing in their regalia and sharing their wisdom. A woman stood up to speak and I was instantly overwhelmed with the realization that I wanted to be like her. Her presence was graceful and self-assured. She introduced herself as a medicine woman and went on to speak of how it is so essential that we all deepen our connections to Mother Earth and treat her with love and respect. After she finished speaking, I summoned up the courage to approach her, knowing that somehow I was about to alter my life path. I asked her, "How does one get to be a medicine woman?" She looked at me with all of the wisdom of the ages and said, "You just have to ask." Her response stumped me a little bit. What did she mean? So, being the straightforward person that I am, I then asked, "Who do I ask?" She gave a little laugh and smiled at me so beautifully. "That's what you have to figure out," she said. I thanked her and walked away, knowing that I had just shifted my life in a huge way, but having no idea at all what it meant. I walked away with the knowledge in my heart that there was someone or something that I could ask. I never doubted that and with the passing of time, cultivated that relationship. I found my guiding voice and I am so grateful for the words of wisdom that led me there.

… # {12}
celebration

> *The thankful receiver*
> *bears a plentiful harvest.*
> William Blake

One of the keys to changing your life story is to believe that it is changing right now. This is not a dream that may or may not happen in the future, it is happening at this very moment. Wake up today and start acting like the new you. You have already been planting seeds for some time. Just by reading this book you are planting seeds. Now is the time to take a good look at what you're harvesting. All of the energy you are putting out into the world is coming back to you in one way or another. What are those ways?

Observe the details of your life. Note how you are inspired and how you lack guidance. There will be a direct relationship between your thoughts and what you are harvesting in your life. But don't dwell on the parts that aren't working. Simply note where you would still like change and figure out how you can focus your thoughts to move in that direction. What will be the next package of seeds you plant?

The best place to take note of the accomplishments in your life is in your relationships with others. The more compassionate and caring you are towards yourself, the more you understand that we all deal with the same issues, in one way or another. We all have moments of not feeling good enough and not being able to respond to others with our hearts. Once you accept that every little thing that has happened in your life has been for a good reason, then there is no longer any reason to go on blaming others for your situation.

With the limitless possibilities of what we can do with our lives, it can be rather overwhelming to try and decide how to spend our time. Do we skydive, knit, race cars, volunteer to feed people, or walk in the country? There may be times when you have to pass up one opportunity in order to follow another, even though your heart wants to do both. That's when it becomes so great that we're really all one being. We don't have to do everything in order for it to add pleasure to our lives. That's what all the other people are for—between us all we can live out a lot of possibilities. We can listen to each other's music instead of having to make our own. We can enjoy each other's cooking without all of us having to be chefs. We can spend our lives caught up in all of the things we've missed out on doing, or we can take pleasure in each other's successes.

We can increase the power of manifesting energy not only by celebrating our own accomplishments, but by celebrating with everyone who experiences success. Don't forget that we are all interconnected. What we give to others comes back to ourselves. Instead of feeling jealous or resentful about the happenings and acquisitions in other people's lives, take their joy to be your own. Really experience what they must be feeling in your own body. This way you are getting to know and be comfortable in a state of elation. Surprisingly, so many of us are not comfortable feeling good, so life doesn't give us too many opportunities to feel that way. Practice feeling good by using other people's lives to inspire you. Send your feeling of joy down to the Earth. She wants to celebrate with you and will be delighted to create more opportunities for bliss.

The more we set our desires for abundance to include everyone, the more we work in line with the Earth's energies. She wants everyone to flourish, not just a chosen few. Yes, there is death and destruction in the natural world, but it feeds an amazing system of order and balance. When we try to segregate ourselves, thinking only about ourselves and how we can be successful, then we are forgetting our interconnectedness. When others benefit, so do you. When you benefit, share your abundance with others. Set your goals for the utmost triumph for all.

Forgiveness is one of the most healing forces in our lives. True forgiveness doesn't mean accepting that someone did you wrong and trying not to let that bother you anymore. True forgiveness is forgiving yourself for ever believing that there was a problem in the first place. True forgiveness is thinking, "Wow. For all those years I believed that there was something wrong with your actions. I have held all that negative energy in my body for so long. I have dwelled in a place of anger and bitterness. Why was I doing that to myself? Holding onto blaming you has hurt me so deeply. I see now that whatever happened between the two of us, it was programmed perceptions of how we thought the other ought to behave. It didn't have much to do with our true selves. I can't blame you for being controlled by your conditioning any more than I can blame myself for that."

We are all in this boat together. We all want to celebrate a bountiful and rich life. Some people (lots of people) have been given a hard time of life and act in ways of which they're not even aware. They struggle within themselves and that struggle is reflected in all of their relationships with others. Some people have been given glimpses of a greater vision of life. They have had moments that clear the way for them to catch sight of their true selves. If we continue to blame others for all of their misguided actions, there will never be true healing in the world.

You have had a glimpse of your true self now. If you look for it, you can't help but find it, however fleeting the moment. Celebrate that part of yourself and encourage it to strengthen and grow. Just like plants need sunlight and water, your true self needs to be nourished with praise and gratitude. Find the opposite thoughts that will guide you to be comfortable in your body. Instead of thinking, "I can't believe I let that person do that to me," try telling yourself how great it was to have that opportunity to learn about human nature and to clarify what you want and need in your life.

Head on down to the harvest dance knowing that every day you are becoming more practiced at using your mental powers to manifest the people, things and situations into your life that are benefitting you and the greater whole. None of us is here in isolation. Whatever energy we are feeling is shared with everyone else on the planet in one way or another. By practicing self-encouragement, you will find yourself naturally encouraging others. That alone is a worthy purpose in life.

Delight in your life and the beautiful person you are. You are living the dream right now; you don't have to wait for some magical thing to happen. Commemorate this accomplishment by making merry and doing some wild visioning about what type of seeds you'll plant next.

We are all everything. If greed exists, then it exists in all of us. By loving the part of you that is greedy, you will be working to heal greed in the world. There are archetypal energies that move in and out of all of us. We need to forgive ourselves for ever believing that there was anything wrong with us in the first place. Then we recognize that everyone is at a different stage on their journey towards awareness. We are able to help heal archetypal imbalances by loving the same traits in ourselves. This is our power. Listen for the core words and love that part of yourself.

It's funny how we can spend our whole lives desperately seeking attention and recognition from the outside world, when we don't even give it to ourselves. It seems so basic to start with ourselves and yet, we are taught that this is egotistical. As we begin to access the voice of our positive thoughts and give ourselves the recognition we deserve, we suddenly start receiving recognition from without as well. Little phrases may come our way that we can hold onto and repeat over and over to ourselves until we believe they're true. If someone tells us that we did a good job, it's so important to believe them. We can't let the voice that wants to say "They're just saying that" have any hold on us.

Step up onto the podium to your place of honour and accept the recognition that is being given to you. Breathe it into your heart and let it settle there. Just as you want others to receive your words as truth, you must be prepared to receive theirs as truth. It is a priceless richness that comes with truly believing that you are a worthy human being, an integral part of the united whole. You can't buy that kind of satisfaction; it must be earned. You have earned it, so don't hesitate to celebrate.

Why is it so much easier to compliment others than to compliment ourselves? Have you been taught that it is vanity if you think anything good about yourself? Whose voice is that? Take the time each day to look yourself in the mirror and tell yourself you look fantastic. Take the time at work to pat yourself on the back for doing a great job. Take time out of your busy schedule to do something that you love to do—do it just for you and for the love of it.

When we have achieved success and celebrated accomplishment, it is important not to settle in and feel like there's nothing more to be done. Each success is a crest, but in the waves of life, it is only temporary. The real trick is to find the balance that allows us to feel motivated to carry on but not be overwhelmed. We don't need to work longer or harder when we are following our true paths. There may be extra demands placed on us now—everyone wants to be a part of what we have going on. Our new found confidence will attract people and while it will open up new doors for us, it may also tempt us to throw the wisdom of our hearts aside and jump into somewhere we don't really want to be. We must maintain our integrity while continuing to nourish ourselves and celebrate our connections with the Earth.

There may be times when you are on the receiving end of blame from someone else. If you get defensive and start arguing, then you will probably miss the message the universe is wanting you to hear. If you accept the blame and carry on to chastise and degrade yourself, then the healing that wants to happen can't take place.

If it feels like someone is attacking you, take a deep breath and do your best to listen to what they are saying without taking it personally. Imagine they are talking to someone else and you are just hearing their words. Try not to react or start spewing out rebuttals—we don't generally express our true feelings very accurately when we're angry. We may hint at them, but it won't be well thought out. Listen for the key words that are being said, though. Take those words away with you and ponder them deeply; see how they relate to you and your feelings. If the other person is saying you're stubborn, love the part of you that is stubborn. If they are suggesting that you blew the deal because you wanted too much, love the part of you that is greedy.

When something does work out for you, make sure you take the time to reflect on how it happened. In gardening, every year is a part of the learning process. By looking back at everything that was done to help nourish the plants—compost, water, sunshine, hoeing—we are able to see what helped and gain insight for how to be better next year. Take stock of what you are doing right and try it again. Think of your life as an experiment and look at it with a curious mind. Take every little factor into account. Once you experience how the little changes you are making inside of yourself are reflected in your outward reality, take credit for your accomplishment. Enjoy the feeling of knowing that you affect your reality. Revel in the fact that you are regaining your personal power.

As we encounter new experiences, we also have the opportunity to create a new way of assessing what is happening. We can fall back into old patterns of criticism and disappointment or we can engage our abilities to be grateful. We can think that we failed miserably or we can give ourselves a pat on the back for giving it our best shot and celebrate all that we learned from the experience.

Fulfillment in your life doesn't happen when you finally have everything you need to be fulfilled, it happens when you are finally satisfied with what you have. It's a deep feeling of knowing that you are taken care of and that there's nothing you can't accomplish, if you set your mind and actions to it. It's knowing that every relationship you have is perfect right now. Being fulfilled is being filled with gratitude. If your goal is to be happy and you realize that the source of happiness is inside of you, then everything else is just icing on the cake. It's harvest time—a time for celebration.

It doesn't matter how small your accomplishments may seem, they are steps toward making your life more fulfilling. Breathe the feeling of success into every part of your body. Even if the only success you can come up with is that you made it through another day, celebrate that. Give yourself permission to earnestly congratulate yourself. Rejoice by treating yourself, knowing that the path you have chosen is one that takes daring and you are a true warrior of life.

The more you practice celebrating your little successes and the little successes of others, when the time comes for your big one, you won't have any hesitation to jump right in and feel at home with being honoured. Sing the thank you song throughout the day. The words are easy. It's just "thank you, thank you, thank you". Make up your own tune. Sing it in your mind and sing it out loud. Sing it as you're driving your car through rush hour traffic and sing it at the end of the day before you go to sleep. Saying thank you means that you are acknowledging that you have received. Singing it often makes it obvious that life is constantly sending little gifts your way.

I love growing heirloom tomatoes. It is so difficult because there are hundreds of different kinds of seeds to start with. At first I must base my decision on just the name and description in a catalogue. Then I get to grow them and see how they taste and how beautiful they are. After the first try, I save the seeds from the cream of the crop—the ones that ripened earliest, the biggest, the ones with the beautiful color. I make salsa, antipasto, ketchup and tomato sauce. I dry some of them. All winter long I deeply enjoy the fruits of my labour. Then the next year I plant those saved seeds, seeds that are now acclimatized to my garden and that I know have certain qualities I desire. The next year my crop is that much stronger and even more beautiful. I have begun to hone my outcome.

Again, I celebrate the harvest by choosing the best of the best to replant the next year. The thing that always amazes me is that by saving the seeds of one small tomato, there is the potential to grow hundreds more. The second year I would be up to thousands more if I planted them all, but I only plant the best of the best to keep it manageable and get excellent results. Come August, I am immersed in tomato deliciousness.

{13}
equilibrium

The best and safest thing is to
keep a balance in your life,
acknowledge the great powers around us and in us.
If you can do that, and live that way,
you are really a wise man.

Euripides

One of the most beautiful outcomes of people awakening the spark of their true selves and becoming more balanced in their lives, is that the balance is also reflected outwards into the state of the world. Indeed, it feels like such a necessary outcome at this time.

There is a certain amount of responsibility that comes with being a conscientious manifestor. If everyone were to fly off in crazy dreams with no regard for how their life affects others, it could get pretty chaotic here on Earth. Without caring about or even paying attention to the effects of our actions, there is no love. Without love there is nothing.

Your heart knows this, and really, you need your heart onboard with you to have a truly magical life. People make things happen every day without being connected to their hearts. Just take a look around. But they aren't living a life of balance and integrity and there is a limit to how far they can go and what they achieve. Without coming from the heart, eventually the scales will tip.

As much as it may seem like we are individual beings on this planet with individual goals and separate means of achieving them, it's not true. There is such a fine web of connection between us all and everything else on the planet that we can't even begin to comprehend it. If you smile at someone and it leads them to smile at someone else, and so on and so on, the effect of one smile becomes exponential. If you take advantage of someone…well, you get the picture. Unless your grand vision is for world sorrow, it's just not likely to work out.

If we are following the conditioned voices in our heads, thinking that they know what is best for us, then we may be mindlessly following old rules and guilt trips. Our hearts know exactly when we are acting in a balanced way in any given situation, moment to moment. Our true, inner voices never mislead us. It may seem sometimes like we're experiencing setbacks, but that's where patience comes in. Balance happens in a smooth, mindful way, requiring no sudden moves in one direction or the other. Doing balance moves in yoga requires every bit of your body to work in unison. Creating balance in life requires the same unity—the unity of your heart and imagination working together.

You'll know when you're slipping out of your heart and back into your head. You'll know because it will feel uncomfortable in your body: a sinking feeling, a knot in your stomach, tightness in your chest, or a desire to get away. That's when we make decisions that we later learn have hurt someone else. That's when we follow paths that don't seem to pan out. We are falling and trying to catch ourselves rather than acting with the confidence of being centered.

This is where simplicity comes into the picture. Imagine the scales so full that there isn't even room to manoeuvre. There is so much of this and that and the other thing, you can't even begin to see which way is up. All of your energy is going into trying not to fall in one direction or the other. When we clean up our lives, both our internal dialogues and our physical surroundings, balance becomes much easier. Everything is more clear. We make room for new energy to enter our spheres when we clear out what is no longer serving us in our lives. We make space to breathe.

Coming into balance in our lives requires a deep commitment to looking at how our actions affect others and the planet, not just now, but for generations to come. The food we eat is a perfect example. Where is the food coming from? How is it produced? What are the repercussions for the Earth? There are people who suggest that you can eat whatever you want as long as you bless it first, but how much blessing will it take to balance out all the effects of chemicals, transportation, slave labour and garbage. We can go along with what everyone else is doing and hope that it all works out alright, or we can become personally responsible. With personal responsibility comes inner peace because you will know in your heart that you are acting for the highest good of all.

Everything we receive comes from Mother Earth in one way or another. It is our responsibility to not just take without giving. The desire to bring dreams into fruition must be balanced with the desire to give thanks and promote life. Listen to your heart to know if your actions are nourishing or depleting.

Clear out the dead weight in your life, be it things you have in your home, relationships that are bringing you down, or negative thoughts rambling about in your mind. Find your solid footing where you can lift one leg, raise your hands to the sky and maintain equilibrium.

Many of us will need to practice giving and receiving. We are so used to doing predominantly one or the other that in order to maintain balance in our lives, we need to be comfortable doing both. If you feel that there is scarcity in your life, you may be better at receiving than giving—fear keeps you from letting anything go because you already feel like you have so little. Try doing something that is a loving act of giving with no expectation for return. There are so many things in life you can give that will cost you nothing. Try giving a smile, a compliment or a helping hand. Give because it feels good to give.

If being comfortable to receive is your challenge, try opening up your heart to let beauty in. Start by receiving from nature. Let the sun shine into your soul and feel in your body what it is like to be a receptacle. You'll have to create space inside of yourself in order to be able to receive. See yourself as the empty vessel that waits to be filled with love. The more you practice receiving, the more you will be able to appreciate and show gratitude for everything that comes your way—even all of the small things that may have gone unnoticed.

When it feels like we are giving more in life than we are receiving, it may be because we aren't truly giving from our hearts. We are giving with the expectation of return. We may be giving what we perceive as our obligations instead of giving a true expression of ourselves. We may be giving begrudgingly. In order to be able to receive with joy, we must be able to give with joy. When we find where our true talents lie and have the confidence to express our higher selves, then delight naturally happens. Delight begets delight in the flow of universal energy.

As we begin to receive more in our lives, it can be easy to fall into a place of wanting to hoard what we have. We are still transitioning out of our ways of scarcity thinking. We haven't found the comfortable expression of "having" in our lives that will put us in a position of being able to give from the heart. Really though, we need to give because we love to give. We need to give because we have already received. Once we are in this flow, it's not going to be cut off. There is no need to fear. Every moment we are receiving the life giving air and sun. Living in a place of gratitude for that alone can put us into a place where we are delighted to share what we have, even if it is the last of something, because we trust in the continuous flow.

If you are finding yourself completely drained because you have been out in the world giving, giving, and giving some more, then you need to remember the principle of balance. Make sure that you allow yourself to be replenished through the things you love to do. If you catch yourself begrudging being such a giving person, that is a good sign it's time to renew yourself.

When we give from our hearts and share the talents we were gifted in the first place, then we're less likely to feel poor. When we appreciate what is and feel content in the moment, then we delight in witnessing others receive. As we give what we have received, we help to restore balance in the world. By offering to others, we strengthen the unified whole and participate in the great exchange of life. Be guided by your intuition and give freely, with no particular expectation for return.

As you find your calling—the work that the universe wants you to do—wonderful new knowledge will come your way. You may discover new mentors that are willing to share what they have learned. Seek out ways to make what you are doing be truly in harmony with the Earth. Make it into something that will benefit generations to come. With the goal of benefiting the Earth and its future inhabitants, you will find that there is always a way to refine yourself and become more in tune with your intuition. As you give thanks for what you do know, more knowledge and insights will come your way, leading you towards mastery.

The wisdom that you accumulate while you inhabit this earthly body will never cease to exist. Just as you have been inspired by the great seers of the past, you will become the inspiration for the generations to come. One day you will be an ancestor and your own unique way of interacting with life will have been added to the wisdom pool.

Your higher self is timeless. There is a dimension where aspects of you have always existed and always will. We fear for our mortal bodies and desire to leave something to show for our time here on Earth. Having children, obviously, is a key way for us to live on through the generations to come, but we don't have to just focus on the physical world. Yes, we can create great works of art that will last some time or businesses that will carry on after we are gone, but we can also make our marks in the universe simply by having creative thought. Every new idea is stored in the Earth's records. Every heart-felt thought that we have echoes through the ages. It goes into building the framework for generations to come. Our stories become a unique volume in the infinite library of life. No one else will ever live the life you have lived, but they will benefit from the truth you discover.

By making your life a story of confidence, success, and happiness, you are putting one more volume onto the bookshelf that others will be able to draw on for generations to come. You are strengthening archetypal energies that know no bounds in time and space. Throughout the ages, people who draw on the wisdom of the past will have your wisdom being whispered in their ear. You will continue to be a guiding force encouraging people to love themselves and share their love with others.

Allow for stillness in your life that you may truly appreciate your blessings. Every one of us is blessed in different ways, every day. Just the fact that we are alive is the greatest blessing of all. As long as we are here, we are creating and have the potential to do great things. The more you can align your heart with gratitude, the more balanced and grounded you will be. You will be open to receiving wisdom. The universe wants you to enjoy life. We can get so caught up in spending all of our time doing and thinking, but that must be balanced with time for just being. Be love and flow in the stream of its beauty.

If you feel like you are living in a world without beauty, make it your mission to supply beauty. If you feel like no one around you has any integrity, cultivate integrity within yourself. When people are caught up in suffering and grief and you wish some peace for them, be the herald of peace. You have the power to bring into the world the things you believe are missing. The world will be transformed by your actions.

While there are things we can do or have that bring us temporary satisfaction in life, so often, when they are gone, the satisfaction is gone, too. We are left with a happy memory, but even that can leave us craving more of the same rather than being content. When we set our sights on the divine aspects of life, we cultivate an inner satisfaction that doesn't disappear in the material world. We are participating with archetypal energies and strengthening their influence for future generations.

I was at an awareness festival one year as a workshop leader. My subject matter was live foods and being spiritually connected with what and how we eat. My workshop the first day was the more practical one, talking about enzymes, sprouting, fermentation and the body's digestive system. After finishing the workshop, I headed to the cafeteria for dinner. I had brought my own food and didn't really want to eat the cafeteria food, but I wanted the opportunity to sit with other people and talk. I could feel the eyes on me as I put a few things on my plate, people wondering what I would have for dinner after my presentation about healthy food options. I knew that whatever I took wouldn't be as pristine as the food in my cooler, but it was serving a higher purpose, so I blessed it and carried on. I ended up sitting at a table with a gentleman who was also knowledgeable about nutrition, spirituality and keeping the body clean. He was eating a big, greasy meal. Another woman at the table asked him about blessing food and he said that he could physically alter the make-up of what he was eating just by blessing it. I sat listening. I believed that was true, but I wasn't convinced it was the whole picture.

I went off to spend some time alone before the dance that evening, still trying to figure out where I stood on the issue. I was supposed to be giving answers in my workshop the next day, but I didn't feel like I knew what the answer was, yet. At the dance, I moved around to the music feeling unsettled. At one point they brought out a big cake to celebrate the festival's 30th year and everyone was so excited. I couldn't bring myself to be excited about a big hunk of white flour and white death sugar, probably with nasty oils and food coloring. I was trying so hard to not judge everyone and curse their beautiful cake, but I wasn't being very successful. I needed some insight. I danced past one of the altars set up around the room with a bowl of angel cards in it. I reached in and pulled out the word "responsibility".

Suddenly it all made sense and I knew what I would say the next day. I said that yes, you can physically change the makeup of the food you eat by blessing it and the more pure you are in your thoughts, the more powerful that blessing will be. But if you direct your blessing to the burger in front of you, you are only affecting that burger. What about all of the other burgers that came from that same cow? So now you bless the cow. But what about all of the land that was depleted so the cow had somewhere to be? So now you bless the land. But what about all the animals and people that were misplaced in the clearing of that land? So now you bless the animals and the people. But what about all of the chemicals and pollution that were involved in getting that burger to your plate? And so on and so on. How powerful is your blessing? How much of your energy are you prepared to put into balancing the scales just so you can eat a burger? The room was silent as everyone looked at me. I told them about how confused I had been the night before and that the universe had given me the word "responsibility" in reply. I didn't need to say anything more.

{14} envision

> *Your vision will become clear*
> *only when you can look into your own heart.*
> *Who looks outside, dreams;*
> *who looks inside, awakes.*
>
> Carl Jung

What is the dream that keeps getting mentioned? Do you have a dream, or are you content to experience each day as it arrives with no thought to the future? That's pretty hard considering we all have things we love to do and would presumably wake up each day wanting to do those things. That in itself is a dream, isn't it?

With your newfound confidence to manifest with your heart comes the opportunity to make your life a really great story. Up until now you've been honing the skills needed to be an effective creator. You've been through cycles of intending and harvesting and are starting to get the idea that this really does work. So what do you want to create? The story can go absolutely any way you want it to go and it can change direction at any time. Keep reminding yourself that there is no limit.

When we get caught up in our minds, our creative thinking tends to be limited to what our narrow belief systems tells us is possible. The true creative potential lies in our hearts. The heart knows no bounds.

It is wild and free. It is joyous to have the opportunity to work together with you on this creative project.

Being in your heart allows you to see your life from a different point of view. It is like the eagle's perspective from high above. Your heart holds the records of all that ever was and will be. It holds the knowledge of everything that is happening right now. Your heart is eager to dream big. Don't try to hold it back.

Once you have an idea of how you'd like to shine forth your gift and share it with the world, whether it be an artistic endeavour, a business enterprise or doing something just for the pure sake of doing it, then it's time to start imagining how you're going to feel once it's accomplished. You've had a taste of the harvest party. Now imagine how you'll celebrate when this new seed you're going to plant comes to fruition. See yourself in a space and look at all of the people who are there in your life to celebrate with you. How does it feel in your body to be this new and spectacular you? How does it feel in your heart?

In order to bend spoons with your mind, it helps to believe that the spoon is already bent. In order for you to manifest your dream, it helps to act like it's already true. There is no doubt of its existence. Every step you take from this point forward leads you to the inevitable reality of your wildest vision. When you move from your heart, your course is straight and true. When you trust your intuition, obstacles cease to impede you.

It's important to not get caught up in the idea of how you're going to make your dream come true. That is the universe's job. Your job is to trust that all of the opportunities you need will materialize before you, waiting to be seized. If you get attached to an idea of exactly how you want your life to unfold, then you are instantly limiting your vision back down to what you now believe is doable. Try to make your vision a bigger picture of what your life will be like and how you will feel, then release your attachment to specific outcomes and let magic take over. Chances are whatever happens will be even better than you imagined.

Life's more fun when you stop trying to figure it all out and just go with it. Imagine how stress free you'll be knowing you are no longer responsible for figuring out how anything in the future is going to happen. All you are responsible for is making decisions in the now. When we try to solve so-called problems with our minds, we can only use what we already know. When we step back and let the master creators handle it, we have only to act wisely in the moment. There is no worry about details, they flow into place.

When thoughts of "How am I going to do this?" start to take over your mind, visualize yourself in the moment of victory. Create a clear picture in your mind. It doesn't matter how it happened. Just feel thankful that it's already underway. Get out of your own way and let the forces of the universe play with you.

What if you really don't know what you want to do? Perhaps you were shut down for trying so many times that you gave up caring. Your heart has a dream. It remembers what it feels like to be brimming with excitement. Think of anything that excites you—even if the best you can come up with is another twinkie. Let the feeling of excitement take over your body. Let it well up inside of you until it just wants to burst forth. Stay with that feeling of excitement. Remember what it feels like so that the next time some bit of an idea pops into your head and you start to feel that way again, you'll recognize it. You'll know that there is something that moves your heart.

Find a vision and try it out. Be prepared to start small and work your way up, gaining confidence with every accomplishment. Be diligent about not letting your self-confidence slip away beneath doubt. Compliment yourself throughout the day on what a great job you're doing. Act towards yourself in the same manner you would want others to encourage you, with excitement and sincerity. Note how many little bits seem to fall into place with ease and grace. Reside in a place of gratitude for all that is.

Is there something you can do to give yourself a taste of what you think you might like, without having to make a full commitment? Go and try on some fancy clothes, even if you can't afford them, just to experience how they feel on your body. Try volunteering with a local organization that is helping people in need, to see if you might enjoy going abroad and offering yourself in service to others. If you think you might like to be a painter, paint. Get out of the box of your daily life and try something new. Even watching movies and reading books about people doing things you're interested in will help to spark your imagination. Envision your story as wonderfully as it can possibly be, then trust that it will be even better. The universe has all kinds of tricks up its sleeve and connections to make things happen. It's not our job to figure out the details of how things will unfold. It's our job to participate with the higher realms in envisioning fulfillment and harmony for all life on Earth.

Being thankful in advance is another great way to remind yourself that on some plane, the vision is already real. Instead of wanting, you will feel satisfaction. Instead of unfulfilled desire, you will have gratitude that it is already so.

Dream your wildest dream; bring your heart on board to live each day in joy as the vision for your life unfolds around you.

When our desires in life don't take the Earth and her inhabitants into consideration, it may seem like we're advancing our goals, but they will never come to full fruition. Your heart cannot ignore the greater good of all because it is clear in its understanding that we are all one, unified life. Only when you create from your heart will you be in balance. So, if you are in a position of trying to figure out what you really want to do for your life to have an impact and bring you joy, take into consideration the talents that you have been born with. The universe already had a vision of your life when you were brought into being. You have had glimpses of what you're really here to do, but perhaps your conditioning has told you that you'll never be able to support yourself or be successful doing it. If you approach your vision from the angle of "what can I give to the world" instead of "what can I take from it", the path to prosperity will be obvious.

Once you have your vision, don't just spread your idea haphazardly to anyone walking by. We function much better when we are surrounded by support as opposed to scepticism. There may be a lot of people in your life who aren't interested in changing their personal story and they certainly aren't interested in hearing you go on about changing yours. That's fine. Let them be. Don't try to convince them of anything.

If you don't have someone in your life you can share your dream with, seek out someone. Anyone who has accomplished what you desire is bound to have words of wisdom and encouragement for you. Because we are all connected, the more people you have cheering you on in your endeavours, the more life force is pushed in that direction. Practice being enthusiastic for others and their dreams—don't limit them in their possibilities—and the same enthusiasm will return for you. Gather together a team of people who are ready to share big dreams.

Whatever you decide to do in life, aim to do your best. Mother Earth always offers us her best; she doesn't try to make more money by making cheap products or try to rip people off by not giving them full disclosure of information. To be respected, you must respect. To receive the best life has to offer, you must put your heart and soul into everything you do. Live a life of quality. Remember that every object you create or idea you put into motion has a life of its own—its own consciousness—and by creating with love you are bringing up the consciousness of the whole planet. Be motivated by the higher award of knowing that you are living your highest expression and that you are a fine craftsman pursuing excellence.

Not everything you dream about is going to happen in your life. Dreaming is like brainstorming—it's about expanding the scope of your imagination so that new ideas can find their way in. If your dream time is spent trying to figure out how you're going to make something specific happen within the current framework of your life, then you're kind of missing the point. Dream big, bigger and even bigger. There is absolutely no reason to limit yourself in dream time. It's an opportunity to try things on and see how they feel. How many times in your life have you thought you knew just what you wanted, but once you got it and lived it for awhile it didn't seem so fulfilling? Our lives are beautiful opportunities to experience, reflect, refine and retry.

The world is full of things to distract us from the business of getting to know ourselves and experiencing our true capabilities as co-creators. We work at pointless jobs in order to fill our emptiness with gadgets and contraptions. Mindless entertainment is pumped into our homes to entice us away from our true callings. We are constantly fed information about how we should look and act, rather than exploring our unique personal expressions. Obligations abound that leave us so drained of life force at the end of the day that all we can manage is to eat something easy and collapse onto the couch.

There's another side of life out there that we're missing—the side that leaves us feeling more energized at the end of the day than at the beginning. There are finer aspects of life that pass by unnoticed. They have the potential to inspire gratitude in our hearts and wonder in our minds. As long as we take direction from the constructs of society, we run the risk of being caught in a stagnant pool. When we start to listen to the voice of inspiration and allow ourselves to be guided by intuition, the realm of possibilities comes into focus and a vision begins to form. Leave behind worldly distractions to fly with the eagle. See a grand picture of life that includes so much more than you've ever dreamed. Allow yourself to move into the direction of fulfillment, uniting with the true scope of the universe.

We all have past experiences that didn't go as we had hoped. Perhaps they left us feeling shattered and beyond repair. We try to hide the pieces deep down inside so that we never have to remember them again—they're so painful. But the bits and pieces of our broken dreams, though it may seem they are the scars of the past, are actually puzzle pieces that will fit into our grand visions. When we have the courage to face pain and transform it, then we free these pieces to fit into place. As long as pain is tucked away, it is like the puzzle piece lost under the couch. The pain doesn't need to be remembered as it is, it needs new life breathed into it. It needs to be loved and touched by the light in order to transform. It needs to be re-remembered with a new twist of compassion and understanding. Then the missing pieces will be revealed and the grand vision puzzle will be that much more complete.

If your desire is for the world to be a happier place but you are dismayed by the darkness that abounds, you don't have to feel overwhelmed or concerned about not knowing how to make a difference. Even if every gesture you make seems to be lost in a sea of oppression, continuing to shine your heart light will make a difference. You don't need to worry about answers; they will be revealed.

Several years ago I was standing in my garden one day in the spring, looking at all of the beautiful flowers and thinking about what an amazing, healing gift they are to the planet. Suddenly a voice popped into my head that said, "Make flower essences of as many of the flowers on this farm as you can, this season." I was rather surprised. I had never made flower essences before. It had never even occurred to me. But the voice had been so clear that I figured it would be in my best interest to follow it. Since I'd been gardening, connecting with nature and using muscle testing more and more, it often felt like the plants were talking to me. So I started making flower essences with no thought of the outcome. It turned out there were way more kinds of flowers growing on our property than I'd realized. By the time I'd done all of the cultivated and wild vegetables, herbs and weeds, I had 132 bottles lined up in rows. But what was next? I ended up creating a book with a description of each essence and now, I use muscle testing to pull out three individual essences, combine them and combine elements of their descriptions to create a unique affirmation. The people that I've made combinations for have been delighted. Often they get goose bumps the first time they say the affirmation out loud, knowing that their life is about to change somehow. My own life has changed dramatically since using them myself. What a gift I was given that day the vision first came to me. With no idea of how it would all unfold or the effects it would have on others, I just knew that it was a vision I wanted to follow.

{15}
the void

Earth teach me to forget myself
as melted snow forgets its life.
Earth teach me resignation
as the leaves which die in the fall.
Earth teach me courage
as the tree which stands all alone.
Earth teach me regeneration
as the seed which rises in the spring.

William Alexander

Letting go of what no longer serves us—there can be a lot of fear attached to this idea. Saying goodbye to parts of you that have been your company through your whole life can feel overwhelming. It means you will have to walk into the place of the unknown.

We want to have our stories in place so that we know what's coming as much as possible. Some people like surprises more than others, but for the most part, we desire a fairly predictable future. This is one of the reasons why we do things the same way over and over again. The new pathways that you are creating in your mind are leading to places you've never been before. They lead beyond your imagination. You are walking each word of the story as it is being written.

In the process of letting one thing go to let something new come in, there is a void you must pass through, the point where there is nothing. Stillness. It is a crack in the universe where anything can happen. We must really want change to have the courage to move through this empty space. We must be willing to accept with an open heart whatever is on the other side.

The seed must crack open in order for the plant to grow. It must cease to be a seed. Are you willing to end life as you know it for the promise of renewal? Are you prepared to see your outer world alter before your very eyes as your beliefs about it change?

Going into the void takes you into a place of no judgement. Our judgements are what we use to orient ourselves in the world. Are you ready to find yourself spinning?

Going into the void means letting go of everything, even the idea that you exist. Perhaps that is why we are so afraid of death, because we don't know if we'll continue to exist or not on the other side. This is only a symbolic death, though. You will continue to exist, only you won't really be that old you anymore, you'll be the new you that thinks differently, talks differently and acts differently. You may even appear differently to yourself and others. Your true colors will shine, making you an inspiration to all.

There are parts of you that will be happy to be left in the void, even though you may occasionally miss them. They are the parts that have been working hard to hold your concept of life together for so long. But they are tired of fighting in some attempt for balance. Just as you have been sending love to all of those parts of yourself—the part that is mean, the part that is angry, the part that is scared—those parts have been receiving your love and they have been finding their peace.

You may find that you used to crave opportunities for confrontation because it was a release for your anger, but now that your angry part is being loved, it has less desire to engage. You may have to reassess your relationships with whomever was on the other side of the confrontation. Either that, or teach them how to love their angry part.

You may find that overwhelming sadness isn't your comfort zone anymore. You're starting to notice too much beauty and joy in all of the things around you to be able to stay sad. As you start smiling more, you recognize that it's actually difficult to feel sad while you're smiling. Music that once touched you may fail to move you. Your favourite movies may not have the same appeal.

It is perfectly great for the anger and sadness of your past to be freed into the void. You may even feel ecstatic. It's not that you're never going to feel that way again; it is the memories that you are freeing, not the ability to feel. When those feelings do come your way, you will support and honour them, instead of feeling like they're shameful and wrong. Be willing to clear the slate with them. Be willing to rewrite the memories that created your belief system. Isn't that what you're here for, to rewrite your story? Any memory that was painful and has left you bitter and angry, rewrite it as being a great learning lesson. Any memory that was sad and has left you disillusioned, rewrite it as a joyous search for compassion.

You are the writer of your story. You have full editing powers, too. Rewrite whole paragraphs so that instead of him going off in a huff, he turned and gave you a hug. Take out the bit about her saying you were stupid and revise it to her offering her support and encouragement. It's your story.

You are not going to disappear by rewriting your story. You are going to reappear. You're going to start to feel whole again. Give thanks to all that has gone before and revel in your new way of being. Breathe in the wisdom that comes with experience and forgive yourself that it took so long to let stuff go. Your vibration is climbing. You'll come out of the void, shining brighter than ever before.

I was driving from Canada to Sedona, Arizona in 2009 to do a week long workshop about opening our hearts. Somewhere in Utah, I ran into an ice storm and had to spend the night parked at a rest stop with all of the other travellers. I had blankets and a mattress set up in the back of my van, but it wasn't enough and I spent the night shivering instead of sleeping. By five in the morning I was so cold, I decided I would just have to drive and deal with it. I had already felt like I was getting a head cold when I left home and now it was really starting to hit me.

Disappointed that it was still dark as I was driving through a "scenic canyon", I went forth bravely. The roads were fine. As the sky started to come back to life, I realized that I was right near Bryce Canyon. I had planned to visit it on my way home, as I needed to be in Sedona that night, but it seemed too tempting that it was right there. I figured if I went that morning, then I'd have the option of going home by a different route. I came over the crest of the hill just as the sun rose over the canyon. It was breathtaking. My head was really starting to hurt and I was very tired, but I decided to go down to the bottom of the canyon. I could see the trail I wanted to be on, winding in and around the hoodoos. This was a long-time dream come true. I asked a fellow if he knew which trail it was and he gave me a name.

Off I went, following the sign for the name he'd said, even though it didn't seem to be going in the right direction. I figured it must wind around somehow. I was so happy, working my way down, down, down, but as I was then going along, along, along, away from where I wanted to be, disillusionment began to overtake me. I realized I had gone the wrong way. I tried to fantasize that there was going to be some great opening in the rock that would take me through the mountain to the other side where my dream was, but I knew it was hopeless. Finally I hit the end of the trail I had been following in a nice but not thrilling valley. I sat down and wanted to cry, but I didn't even have the energy for that. So instead, I meditated, sitting on a rock beside the flowing water with the sun shining on me and the wind blowing softly. "If I'd been in the other valley, I wouldn't be in the sun," I thought. "Maybe this isn't so bad."

Then I got up to start walking back, remembering that I still had to drive all the way to Sedona. I'm from the Kootenays where I hike up first, and then come down. As I stood at the bottom of the canyon and looked up to where I needed to be, I knew I was in trouble. All I wanted to do was lay down in the sun and rest. Already my legs did not want to walk, but somehow I had to get to the top. Part of the workshop I was going to was about connecting to Mother Earth and Father Sky, so I looked to them for renewal. I let go of all my thoughts of defeat and despair and kept one foot moving in front of the other. Each time I looked up to a spot part way up the canyon, I imagined myself already there, waving back down at myself, encouraging me on. I made up a song to Earth and Sky and just kept singing to keep my intention pure. I've spent my life pushing my physical limits through dance, sport, and manual labour, but never had my body cried out to stop the way it did that day. I dug deeper and deeper to find new stamina that I didn't know I had.

Finally I reached the top and looked back down at where I'd come. I could see all of the places where I had let go of the parts of me that were not going to get me to the top. I thanked Mother Earth and Father Sky with a newfound connection that could not have happened any other way. I looked down again into the canyon where I had originally wanted to be and thought, "It's just eye candy." Knowing that I would never return to be who I was just four hours ago, I got into my van and drove.

{16}
intermingle

Everyone thinks of changing the world,
but no one thinks of changing himself.
Leo Tolstoy

If you think about the ingredients in your favourite dish and separate them, chances are, the thought of eating any one alone isn't as appetizing as eating the delicious whole. Blending things together is what gives us a rich life. It creates new things and new ideas.

When we are in relationship with others, there is a blending that goes on between us—a space where we overlap. Have you ever found that after having spent significant time around a person, you both use the same expressions? There is a blending of stuff that happens when two or more people share a space, be it physical, emotional or spiritual. If there isn't, then it means there are big walls up. Think of the difference between two circles side by side and two circles overlapping.

With the cleansing of our thought patterns, there's bound to be a new set of priorities revealed. Things that once mattered, won't any more. New ideas may catch your eye, things you'd really like to try. What is the blend of this new you?

There is no limit to the possibility. Keep reminding yourself that. No limit.

How do you want to spend your time? Who are the people you're overlapping? It's just like writing a book; start answering the questions that need answering. There will be characters, presumably, each with their own unique set of traits. There will be times when emotions run high and times of rest and recovery, preferably with fabulous scenery. Think about what makes a good story, one that you would actually like to live.

When the pen touches the paper, there are no restrictions. There's nothing that can't happen. It's no more difficult to make a big dream come true than a little one. Why go small? Write something epic for your life. Write a story about really enjoying being you. Blend together all of the parts of you that you enjoy, the parts that feel good in your body.

Let your heart be the master chef. You are the prep cook who gathered the ingredients. It's time to let go now and watch the master perform. A bit of this, a splash of that, let's throw in a dash of whatever because it makes people smile. Allow your heart to bring forth your inner amazingness. Be prepared to shine.

Take a deep breath and look around your shining self. You'll begin to notice there are other shining people all around you. Overall vibration has gone up a notch. There are people around for whom you genuinely care and you go out of your way to help. There are people who don't come to you with problems, they come to you with wonderful ideas. There are animals that are your dearest friends and plants that nourish you.

Now you're not afraid to let them into your space, to let them overlap with you a little bit. Now we're serving one dish with another and some lovely wine and scrumptious dessert. Our world has become delicious.

What are you going to accept into your new story? There are ingredients that you've never even heard of before. There are ingredients that don't even exist until you call them into being. You don't have to commit right away. Start with a nibble and see what you think. Just because someone else says it's their favourite, doesn't mean it's going to be yours. You need to spend time with it to see how it makes you feel.

Take time in your life to experiment with new combinations. What happens if you walk around smiling all day? Other people will react. What happens if you decide, just for today, one particular part of your life is not going to cause you any stress? Maybe you'll decide to try something similar again tomorrow—a little less or a little more. Then again, maybe not.

You gain confidence in your life. It is a wonderful gift to share your knowledge with others walking a similar path. Remember that there was a time when you were looking for inspiration and wisdom, seeking out the masters. Even if you are far from being a master yet, you still have much to share with others. Through sharing, you will be opening yourself up to receive even more insight and new ideas. Don't try to force your knowledge on anyone who is not ready to receive it. Guide and provide for others as a loving presence.

As we clean up our thoughts and bodies for a deeper connection with life, we feel an increase in energy and excitement. It's like being at a sports game. As each play takes our team further into the lead, we move to the edge of our seats. We feel the power that comes with winning as it surges within us.

This is the time when it is most important to remain centered in our hearts. This is the time when it may be tempting to throw a vision of helping the world aside and just go for the gold. New found wealth may tempt us to spend our money foolishly. New found confidence and attraction may lead us into relationships that are not serving our higher selves. Feeling invincible, we may throw aside all of the discipline we have cultivated with regard to our bodies and our health.

Excitement can lead us to make rash decisions rather than to walk with balance, patience, and integrity. We must maintain the inner peace that keeps us in touch with intuition. We can put these powerful feelings to good use by letting them feed motivation, rather than desire for gratification. Yes, there will be plateaus reached and genuine reasons to celebrate success, but they are not the stopping point. We can always seek higher visions and find more ways to give back and to give thanks.

Don't be afraid to let the changes that you are making inside reflect how you are around other people. If they think you're wacky, then maybe it's time to let them go. Remember that this world needs more people like you—people who care about being a connected part of the universe instead of ignoring it. Present a harmonious blend to the world and keep on smiling.

When I was a teenager, I was pretty depressed most of the time. The only thing that kept me going was dance class after school every day. When I was dancing, I was free from my thoughts, totally engaged with my body and experiencing joy. I didn't smile much in my life during those high school years, and people really noticed. I was constantly getting told to "smile", even by strangers on the street, which just made me grimace more. I had a nice smile. I suffered through years of wearing braces to have nice straight teeth, but when I was caught up in my head, I couldn't find the joy needed to inspire me to beam.

At college a few years later I was beginning to come out of my depression. My boyfriend introduced me to a whole underground movement of thought and music that gave me hope that the world was more than what I had been taught. It was my statistics professor one day who called on me in class by saying, "You, the one with the nice smile." He actually said that to me in front of a class of about 100 people. I was floored. A new little part of me woke up.

Several years later, when I was a tree planter and becoming even more aware that I could make my life into anything I wanted, I was leaning against the wall in a crowded bar, watching with amusement the antics going on around me. Someone approached me and said, "What are you smiling about?" I'm smiling because that's what I choose to do, I thought. I'm smiling because that's who I am now.

{17}
enticement

*The biggest human temptation
is to settle for too little.*
Thomas Merton

As we blend together new and amazing versions of ourselves, it can be rather daunting that we really can choose to believe anything we want. Human beings have free will—free meaning limitless and will meaning the ability to make choices. But so many of our choices have been made from subconscious programming that it can be like cleaning up a dusty attic to find our personal truths.

There are bound to be things we believe to be true that just aren't true. In some cases, it may take a lot of convincing for us to let go of old beliefs. We don't want to admit that we've been wrong about things, especially those of us that have stood so strong in our convictions and been so outspoken with our opinions.

Lots of ideas that aren't true can be well-disguised. They can be tempting. After all, everyone around you seems to believe it. Regardless of how it is that certain beliefs become popular opinion, it doesn't mean they are true.

What is truth, anyways? Is it something you know beyond a shadow of doubt? A dictionary definition says it is something that is in accordance with fact or reality, but who is the ultimate voice that says that something is fact; isn't reality a matter of individual perception? The point is that the only voice that can decide for you what is true and what isn't true, is yours. That's the beauty of limitless possibility. It's also the challenge.

Wise people understand that letting go of their belief that they know anything to be true is a huge step towards living an authentic life. Believing that we know "the truth" can lead to judgement, anger and disappointment. It leads to isolation. It draws a line between you and others and keeps you from being free.

Just as you use your words to create what you want in life, so do others, but they don't all do it with harmony and balance in mind. People will tell you all sorts of things in order to sell you something or make you act a particular way. They may even believe what they are saying, but that doesn't make it the truth. If your feelings are incongruent with what you are hearing, take that as a sign to dig deeper. If what you are being told will have an overall harmful effect on life, you may want to reconsider. Don't be tricked into believing. Make time and space in your life to ponder and discover your personal truth.

So often we base truth on past experience. If something has happened a certain way before, then we assume that it will happen that way again. We end up living a life that seems to be moving forward but is really a constant repeating of the past. Where is the life in that? With an endless sea of prospects, why limit yourself to what has gone before?

Everything that has ever happened to you to limit your perception of potential is stored away somewhere in your thinking. The sooner you accept that each of those experiences was only "one possible way" and not "the only way" life can be, the sooner you will fly with your free will. The more you work to recreate those memories, to know the beauty and benefit of them, the more you will see that believing things to be "true" can be a trap. You'll release yourself from the confines of your thinking.

You may experience resistance from others who are feeling safe in their boxes. They may try to convince you that you are wrong, that they know what is best for you. You may have to ask yourself the same questions over and over again, searching for a new answer each time, to really get to the bottom of things. You're going to have to take a good look at what you've been told and what you have formulated from the results of your observations. Leave no rock unturned.

There is no need to blame anyone or anything for having misled you in life. Everything that happens just is—it's not right or wrong. After all, if you hadn't received the conditioning you did, in the unique way that you received it, you wouldn't be the you that you are at this very moment, deciding to do something to change your life. Everything that has happened to you has been a gift, no matter how difficult it is to believe.

There is no need to blame yourself for having allowed yourself to be conditioned. It's a natural part of how we learn to observe, listen, and put together cause and effect. As young children, it keeps us safe to fit within the constructs that surround us, but we are no longer children and our spirits yearn to be free. In order to change the construct we exist within, we must first change our beliefs. If we wait for outside reality to change to make us happy—a better job, a more loving spouse, a healthier body—we may be waiting for a long time. Change has to come from within.

Our belief systems are like the many layers of an onion. As we peel away one layer of concepts, it reveals another. When we think we have discovered a truth, we may realize that there are so many more levels to work through. At the center of the onion is your pure, shining self—a being beyond truth.

Our thoughts are the way we give order to reality. They are perceptions, not reality itself. If you ask two different people what happened at a particular moment in time and space, their answers may be slightly different. Their answers may be completely different. They may not even agree on what words were actually said. Everyone hears what they want to hear to support the story they are creating. The event itself doesn't even actually exist. Only the memories exist of the people who were present and their memories have been tailored to fit into their own concepts. Trying to argue about what happened in the past is futile because there isn't one truth.

Of course we are going to make mistakes in life, that is how we learn. If we always did everything perfectly, it would probably mean that we are never trying anything new or pushing our own limits. There would be no growth. Things that are alive need to grow. Just as the compost that makes the plants grow is made up of old plant material that has broken down, our mistakes are composted into rich soil to feed our spirits and help us mature. Give thanks for your mistakes, get back up on that horse and appreciate the new wisdom that is yours.

Saying affirmations may feel silly at first because most of us have not been trained to think in such ways. But really, the fear of sounding cheesy is just a fear of experiencing divine ecstasy. It's the fear of the unknown; it's resistance to experiencing yourself in all of your power. Once you've done it enough that poetry flows through your mind, instead of angst, the spiritual highs will make you wonder how you could have been afraid to feel so good.

If you think you know what has been blocking you from getting the results you desire in your life, but you're still not experiencing any change, then it's time to go back to the drawing board and dig deeper this time. Really listen to the words that want to pop into your head. Make sure you're not cutting yourself off from thinking any thoughts because those will be the ones that are still hindering you. Our minds have a lovely way of not wanting to reveal their inner workings. They want to maintain control, but can't help letting stuff slip now and then. Listen to the questions you ask yourself and look for your hidden fears.

If you find that your mind is prone to jealousy, find some diversion tactics to steer you out of it. The first step, of course, is to actually listen to your own thoughts and realize that you are dancing with the green monster. You have to want to change it. Then, force yourself, no matter how much you resist, to find something positive to think about the person. Don't allow your mind to go back to the topic of your jealously. Seek out something good to think. Either that, or forget about them all together and find some reason to praise yourself, instead. Don't base the praise on you being better than the other person, base it on your genuine gratitude for what you are. You aren't like them and they probably have things that you don't have, but so what. You are both shining beings of light with a plethora of talents and kindness to share.

When I was in my early thirties, I began to wonder why I wasn't married yet. The best explanation I could come up with was that no one had ever asked me. I decided this was my truth. So, it's not surprising that not long after that I met a guy who seemed to fulfill my ideal. He was introduced to me through people that I loved and trusted, he had a good job and prospects for the future, and within three months he asked me to marry him. I didn't hesitate to say yes, believing that the universe had given me exactly what I wanted. I was feeling pretty darn good about my manifesting powers and began planning my dream wedding and a life of happiness. It didn't take long for weird little moments to start happening that made me question what was going on. I began to feel uncomfortable around him. I started to realize that I actually didn't know him at all and that whatever I had believed to be true about him wasn't really.

One day I found myself walking down by the river, feeling completely despondent. I knew that I couldn't carry on forward with the relationship, let alone get married, and that I had to get myself out of this situation—a situation I had gotten myself into by thinking I was so smart and knew it all. That evening I had to face the blow-out as I returned his ring and broke up with him. Needless to say, he didn't take it very well. By the time I left his house, I was shaking all over. As I walked through the brisk, evening air, back towards my freedom, I could feel layer after layer of limiting beliefs blowing away in the breeze. Then I knew my truth: it was never about the universe giving me a husband, it was about the universe giving me the opportunity to learn how to get out of uncomfortable situations. I found a strength inside of myself that I hadn't known—a strength that was my truth.

{18}
obliteration

*Every act of creation
is first an act of destruction.*
Pablo Picasso

So, here we are, realizing that truth is a vaguer concept than we believed. The laws of life are not written in stone and we have the ultimate creative power to design our own truths. You may walk out onto the street, look around and realize that nothing is what you thought it was—even you are not what you thought you were. You are standing on a blank, white page, holding the pen in your hand that has the ability to invent a whole new life.

This can be pretty daunting. Our old beliefs created a structure to work within and that structure is falling to pieces. Having clearly defined sets of societal and religious values has kept us from having to really think individually about life. They have given us groups to belong to, formats to follow and scales on which to rate ourselves and others as good or bad.

When you truly embrace that there is no limit to what you can believe, everything comes into question. As the layers of the onion peel away, even things you believed as true, without a doubt, may come up for reconsideration. It will become clear how many of your actions are motivated by guilt. The realization that you are acting certain ways only because you believe you should, may lead you to question the very nature of existence.

Although scary and new, what a great place this is to be. As you clear away the debris of your past conditioning, the voice of your true self will become much more than a mere whisper. It will become a clear, guiding force. You may think that you're headed into a place of confusion and difficulty, a place where you are all alone, but you will really be more connected than ever.

People sometimes talk about their awakening life moments as being hit over the head with understanding, or blown away by the truth. Moving through the place of emptiness between where one idea existed and a new one begins to form leaves you, for a moment, in the void. Glimpsing the profound marvel of pure potential and feeling it in your body as a release of so much old, contained energy, may knock your socks off. It may even seem like life isn't going your way, as your palette is cleared. The universe may be one step ahead of you in providing opportunities for growth. Amazing things happen as soon as we ask for change in our lives. As soon as we acknowledge divine connection to the source of all possibility, new forces come into play. One of the biggest things that has been holding us back is the belief that we are individuals and alone in making things happen.

You are an individual only as far as you are one bit of divine spark that is able to set things into motion, but everything you create in this life is part of the greater whole. Every action has a reaction and every cause has an effect. When you change, your world can't help but change around you. Isn't this the point? Aren't we doing this because we want to change our lives?

In order for the river to change its course, it must break down the earth in a new direction. In order for food scraps to break down into compost, there must be destruction. How far are you willing to go to make changes in your life? Are you ready to step into the unknown?

Luckily, for most of us, we don't just suddenly have a huge epiphany that shakes our lives to pieces. The clearing of old beliefs is a gradual process that cultivates patience and understanding. Sometimes big things happen to people that force them to radically reassess their lives, but even then it may only be one aspect of their lives—their work, relationship or health. The universe is here to support us in this process, not to leave us begging for mercy.

We can start by working with our beliefs about who is in control of our lives to awaken inner power. We can look at our concepts of good and bad to realize we are all shining, deserving beings. Next, we look at our beliefs about abundance so resources flow more freely. We give thanks for all that is. Follow that with a look at beliefs about being alone and unsupported and the need to worry fades away.

There are so many areas of life to reassess, it may take years or even a lifetime. Are you spending your time where your talents lie, doing what you love? Who and what are you spending your time with and how real is your connection? How confident are you to express your personal truth to others? How many of your beliefs are blocking the flow of energy in your life rather than enhancing it?

You may come up with a new set of beliefs one year, then reassess them again the next year when you still aren't getting the desired results. You may have to ask yourself what the truth is, over and over again, as new information and insight comes your way. All along the way, your light will shine brighter, giving you the protection you need from doubt, both self-doubt and criticism from others.

Recognizing that there are no problems, only opportunities, makes it much easier to deal with big life changes. Grounded in the knowledge that we have everything we need inside of us to deal with any situation, we are able to cope with things that may previously have left us incapacitated. Yes, life may still be overwhelming and scary, but we have the tools we need to deal with it. We may even catch ourselves enjoying the ride. Fear is transformed into excitement, knowing that we are supported through difficult times and that our lives falling to pieces is a sign that they are about to be rebuilt.

Trying to build something new on top of an old foundation is always going to be a limited experience. There will be new aspects, but the basic structure will still have the same dimensions. If you want a new story, be prepared to start from scratch. That means you have to be prepared to let go of everything you've ever thought to be the truth. Knock it all down and start sifting through the rubble to find what has survived. Question each belief you allow back into your framework and be prepared to find creative ways for them to fit together.

As the story of your life is recreated, be willing to let your known structures fall away. Keep breathing and loving and from the blank page the words will begin to form a most miraculous story—the story that can only be written by you in all of your uniqueness.

LEGEND THAT YOU ARE

There is an idea that if we feel bad about what is going on in the world, then all we are doing is adding to the overall bad feeling. This seemed to make sense to me, but I hadn't had the opportunity to experience how significantly the idea would play out in my life. Then in 2004, there was the huge tsunami in the Indian Ocean.

The devastation was inconceivable from my Canadian point of view. It seemed that the whole world was in a state of mourning. I thought about the idea that if I joined in with feeling bad, then I wasn't actually participating in bringing joy back to the world. I tried to take a deep breath and feel a generic happiness and was immediately overwhelmed with guilt. The thought that popped into my mind was that if I was feeling happy when something so terrible had happened, didn't that make me a bad person? "Good" people were feeling the wreckage as deep sadness. I took another breath and tried again. Yes, I actually felt bad that I wasn't feeling bad. I wondered how deep my guilt conditioning went and if I'd ever be able to get past it. I had always thought of myself as a good person. Was I going to have to go through being a bad person in order to get to the place of being a true person? My whole concept of myself was going to have to be shattered.

I took one more breath and tried, just as an experiment, to feel joyous and thankful for the Tsunami. I was so happy that my friend who was in Thailand had been on the last boat that made it safely to the shore before the waves hit. I was inspired by how the survivors would be bonding and forming new, deeper relationships. I was delighted that new systems and structures would be put into place that would be an improvement on what came before. I wanted to break down sobbing because of how difficult it was and how awful it felt to try and feel some joy about the situation, but I knew in my heart that joy was what the world needed right then, not more suffering. I knew that I needed to get past my own conditioning that I was a bad person for not feeling bad and strive to be a shining light.

{19} wisdom

*Look deep into nature,
and then you will understand everything better.*
Albert Einstein

Moving through the void, accepting that every single thing you believe is up for question, and discovering the place inside of your heart of pure stillness with no emotional obligation, leads to an amazing thing happening. You no longer operate as a separate identity that is composed of a seemingly endless list of beliefs. You remember that you are a unique and connected part of a whole that is so great we can't even begin to fathom its magnitude.

With this newfound connection comes foundations and support from the greater whole that were previously ignored. Our eyes open to the subtle ways that life operates around us and we begin to see the opportunities and support we are given. We recognize the little things that happen each day—a word here, a look there, the perfect parking space.

We feel the energy of the land and remember that there have been people, plants and animals living here for generation upon generation. Every experience that has ever happened on this planet is stored in a grand, eternal memory. Every answer that we may ever need already exists. We just need to know what questions to ask.

As conscious creators, we have the wonderful ability to choose a sacred path that will uplift the vibration of the whole planet. We are given the free will to discover where our unique talents lie and use them to make the world a better place. When the consciousness of humanity is raised, it affects every living thing on this planet. It affects the sun and the moon and the stars. It influences other dimensions and even other times. What better incentive to deepen your connection with all life than knowing you will be playing an integral part in creating more joy?

One of the best ways to deepen your connection with the natural world around you is to eat locally grown food as much as possible. If you think about it, native populations were literally made from the land where they lived. Other than small amounts of trading, everything they consumed came from the earth that surrounded them. Their very cells were made of the same minerals as the trees and the birds where they lived.

So much of our disconnection with nature these days comes from eating foods from all over the world. One meal can literally contain energy from every continent on the planet. Where you live has its own unique vibration. The more you align with that vibration, the better you will be able to hear the wisdom of the trees in your yard.

A great way to show respect for all life is with lovingly prepared food. If we see eating as a chore, it will not nourish us. If we begrudge having to spend money on food, we are eating that resentment. When we take the time to enjoy the colours, tastes, and textures of everything we consume, we share that enjoyment with the Earth and honour the fact that she is feeding us. The food we eat has consciousness, too. Ask yourself if you are uplifting your vibration with what you eat or acting like it is simply fulfilling a requirement in your life. Are you giving back your thanks or simply taking?

We have become so disconnected from our ancestors and the natural world around us. If you have been raised in the city, you may never have experienced the peace that comes with being silent in nature. Perhaps you have never known the exhilaration of climbing a mountain and being on the top of the world. These experiences open you up in ways that nothing else can.

Nature is full of metaphor. When we take time to observe the miracles that go on around us every day, we awaken the part of us that has been living in tune for eons. We understand what the real questions are and we begin to know the answers. What seemed like problems becomes insignificant in the shade of a tree that has been growing for hundreds of years. What felt like obligations becomes opportunity in the dappled light of the grove. Our very cells become calm as our priorities become clear.

When was the last time you read some great poetry or a book from the past that totally inspired you? We tend to feel like the times we live in are unique and that the wisdom of the past is somehow outdated and inconsequential, but it is an accumulated understanding that has withstood the test of time. Seek out the knowledge of the ancestors who could still hear the voice of the natural world and listen to what they have to say. This knowledge is more relevant than ever before because it will help lead us back to a place of balance.

Surround yourself with the wisdom of the ages. There is a reason particular combinations of words have survived throughout time. They still ring true and they speak to the enlightenment of all life. When you need some reassurance that you are on the right path, or you need some insight or inspiration, look to the words of the poets and storytellers.

When was the last time you sat on the beach and held a stone or a shell in your hand? What happens when you sit without expectation or distraction and listen without judgement to the thoughts formulating in your mind? All of the knowledge of the universe is held sacred in every stone and crystal. The wind in the trees speaks with the voice of ancient insight.

The way nature speaks to you will be unique. Not everyone who sees a red-tailed hawk fly overhead will have the same experience. While there are universal symbols, such as the dove for peace, everyone lives life in their own personal way. Don't try to seek out someone else's opinion as to the meaning of what you experience. Go inside of yourself, to your stillness, and notice what comes to your mind. Let what you observe trigger an opening in yourself to reveal your hidden wisdom. Maybe whatever you see is just aiming to bring your attention back to the present so you don't miss the next important thing that's going to happen; a bird call makes you look up and notice the person across the street, or stopping to smell the roses takes you out of the path of an accident that is about to happen. Always trust that life is unfolding perfectly around you with your best interests at heart.

Spending time in nature allows you to remember that you, too, are a part of nature and that you, too, already hold all of the answers that you seek. Every cell in your body holds all the information of infinity. There is no fence dividing you from Mother Earth. She is your mother and you have received all of her genetic coding. There is nothing she won't share with you with an open heart.

Every life that has ever been lived on this planet is a part of you. As a human being you are given full access to the files of information that are stored in the rocks and the water, the wind and the trees. All memories went into making you and your heart knows no bounds. Every living thing is talking to you, always. Every thing that happens around you is significant. Every question that you have is already answered. You just need to listen.

The more time we spend in nature, opening ourselves up for communication, the more we recognize that consciousness resides in everything. It can be easier to recognize it in animals, but the plants and even the earth itself are all part of this interwoven, ultimate being. They hold the wisdom of the ages like anything else. The more we are able to honour all life by choosing our actions based on how they affect everything, the more connected we become to that innate wisdom and the clearer its communications.

When you stand with your feet on the ground in a place where the ancestors lived in harmony with Mother Earth, you feel the power that remains in that place. The voices of wisdom will be strong and they will want to talk with you. Everybody that has been buried after death has decomposed and become part of the earth again, the earth you stand on. Every breath that has ever been taken has moved in and out of countless life forms, regenerating and recycling. If you have the opportunity, try visiting any of the sacred sites around the world. Experience the deep connection that is part of our history. Remember that all wisdom is yours, if you ask.

Just because a belief system that people are following doesn't seem to be benefitting the whole, doesn't mean that there aren't grains of truth within it. Not everything you were taught as a child will be limiting. You already have a vast wealth of wisdom within you. You must keep questioning, though. Just because a belief system has been around for thousands of years doesn't make it perfect. In fact, the only belief system that will be perfect for you is the one you create yourself. Seek out bits and pieces from the ancient ways and the Earth and weave them into your own unique tapestry.

When I was in Arizona, I had the amazing opportunity to attend a Full Moon Medicine Circle with one of the elders of the Havasupai. There was a fire in the center of the circle and we all smudged as we entered the sacred space. We sang songs to welcome the energies of the seven directions and to join our hearts together in a common desire. Then the elder began to walk in a circle around the fire. He walked and he walked while he spoke the wisdom of his ancestors and his own unique understanding of reality. Just listening to the tone of his voice and the rhythm of his words while the firelight flickered off his regalia drew us into an otherworldly place where we, too, were connected with the heart beat of Mother Earth and Father Sky. He spoke of how every little thing that surrounds us in our lives, from the bird on the wire to the ways of the weather, is Mother Earth speaking to us. He told us that it is time to listen to the voice of spirit. The best way we have of honouring the Earth and living a life of integrity is to listen. At the end of the evening, I shook his hand and felt such a deep connection with wisdom. His words awoke a place inside of me that knows that there is no difference between me and him and the Earth. I am the eagle flying high and I am the fish in the sea. There is nothing that I am not.

{20}
inklings

*You have to leave the city of your comfort
and go into the wilderness of your intuition.
What you'll discover will be wonderful.
What you'll discover is yourself.*

Alan Alda

Just as there is information constantly coming to us from the natural world and the wisdom of our ancestors, there is information coming to us from the pure spirit that we are. We call it intuition. Some people believe that some of us are intuitive and others aren't, but really, we all have access to this innate wisdom, some of us are just better at listening to it than others.

Our bodies contain immense creative potential and our spirits want us to follow our intuition in a creative way. If you are standing in an art gallery and your intuition tells you that you, too, could be a great painter, don't listen to the voice saying that you're not good enough to do that. If your intuition is telling you to get up off the couch and go for a walk, do it. Perhaps you're going to run into the exact person you need to connect with in order to move forward with your career. Your intuition may egg you on to move when you're feeling stuck.

On the other hand, your intuition may be the voice telling you not to go and confront the person you're angry with right now. It may direct you to explore your angry feelings alone and let them metamorphosis. Your intuition may be the one trying to stop you from going out driving in the rain to some function that you feel obligated to attend. It may be trying to keep you safe.

Following your intuition can be so rewarding. It can be like little miracles happening every day. You buy the gift for your friend that isn't what you would normally choose but turns out to be exactly what she wanted. You turn down the promotion at work and the next week the perfect job for you becomes available.

Intuition is the very first sense you get about something, but it is amazing how quickly it can be overridden by all of the should-voices in your head. It can be overpowered so easily that you hardly even know it's there. It can be the thought that was only beginning to form to find the words to express itself before doubts and insecurities send it back to the ether.

Many times your intuition will only have a chance to be known as a feeling in your body. Your heart will be trying to tell you something even though your mind doesn't know how to listen. Your pulse will quicken and you'll get a tight feeling in your chest or stomach. You may even sweat. You may remember this happening to you as an experience of "it didn't feel right, but I did it anyway." You may remember that more often than not, it is when you went ahead anyway that it didn't work out so well.

Some people hear the voice of intuition and still choose to ignore it, for whatever reason. Maybe it's because their social conditioning says something else. Maybe it's because intuition is telling them to take the harder route and they feel lazy. Or maybe they don't believe that they truly have access to the wisdom of right action. Often we ignore intuition because it is speaking the answer that is for the greater good of all and we don't see how it's going to benefit us personally.

We keep trying to push the voice of intuition away so we can get on with our lives and what needs to be accomplished for our basic survival. What we end up doing is breaking ourselves down so far that it becomes a huge struggle to be able to put ourselves back together again. We ignore all of our higher needs until we are little more than robots maintaining the status quo. Eventually the robot breaks down and we are left with nothing.

Ignoring intuition leads to a build-up of misinformed concepts. These ideas actually reside and accumulate in our bodies, leaving us sluggish and cloudy. Think of your sink's drain. If you are only ever running clear water down it, the pipes will remain clean and the water will always flow freely. If you keep dumping coffee grinds and carrot peels down the drain, eventually you will have a drainage problem. The water will no longer be able to flow freely. The sluggishness that builds up in our bodies will eventually make itself known as disease.

But your body always knows the best course of action. It knows to pull your hand away when something is hot. It knows to stand back a bit from the edge of the big drop-off. When you are meeting someone for the first time, your body knows whether or not to trust them. Your body knows whether the way you feed it and treat it are beneficial. Unfortunately, we've been taught to ignore the feelings in our bodies.

We cover up discomfort with pain killers. We alter our cycles with hormones. We numb our emotions with pharmaceuticals.

Intuition is the knowledge that actually makes our lives easier. Being in tune with infinite wisdom brings ease and grace into our lives. Instead of struggling against the current, trying one thing after another that doesn't work out, we flow with the universe and are supported in all of our endeavours. Our cells are constantly being rebuilt with the energy of joy and self-confidence instead of being broken down by doubt and despair.

Sometimes following intuition requires great patience. We want everything to occur right now and so we go against better judgement just to have something happen. But if we had waited, the perfect experience for us was just around the corner and now we're headed in the opposite direction. Now we've got to go around the block three more times to get back to the place of perfect opportunity once more.

Your intuition knows when to act and it knows when to wait. If you are unsure, try standing solidly on your two feet, centered and grounded. Ask your higher self if you should move forward or not. Free the movement of your body and see if you are drawn forwards or backwards. This is a simple form of muscle testing that will help guide you in making all kinds of decisions, from what to eat to where to go. Your body already knows the path of least resistance and highest good.

Your intuition will speak to you in many ways and the more clear your mind is of babble, the more you will be able to hear it and believe it—the more you will trust it. Words will float into your consciousness, music will inspire you, and your body will gently guide you. Trust that you are a part of something much grander than yourself, an energy force that wants you to succeed and share your creative gifts with the world. Trust that you are not alone and that a path is being cleared for you with every step you take. The miracles you desire are ready to happen now.

Intuition is spirit moving through you. When you don't allow your intuition to influence your decisions, you are shutting yourself off from a whole aspect of your being. Intuition works through your body—a feeling in your gut. If you are disconnected from your body, there's another aspect of your being that isn't being considered. Intuition speaks through your emotions—something just doesn't feel like a good idea. So often we ignore our emotions because they have left us too vulnerable in the past. Take out your spirit, your body and your emotions from your operating system and you haven't got much left—a mind that isn't even really you. Intuition is your connection with life. Allow it to sing its song and trust that it is a benevolent voice seeking the highest good for all.

It can be scary to act on your intuition because so often it will inspire you to do something you've never done before or something that goes against the way everyone else is doing things. But isn't that what this is all about? Aren't we trying to create change? As long as we stay within our comfort zones, all we do is maintain the status quo. It can be frightening to make a move without knowing we will be supported, but the moment we take that first step in a new direction, reality will shift. It can't stay the same.

If you are in doubt about which path to take, muscle test. Your higher self wants you to be able to follow its lead and accept its gifts, so it will always direct you helpfully. When you're standing grounded and connected, you will naturally be drawn toward that which benefits you the most. Muscle test for anything and everything. Which toothpaste to use? Take the freeway or the back roads? Say that out loud or not? We don't have to be confused by life and feel like we don't know which way to go or what to do. All the information we need to make wise decisions is at our fingertips. We just have to ask.

Many years ago, I discovered the wisdom of the runes and decided to collect some polished stones off of the beach to make my own set. I randomly choose 25 stones and laid them out before me. Not knowing how to choose which rune to write on which stone, I decided to just start doing it and see where my eye and hand led me. With each rune I chose the stone that for some vague reason seemed appropriate. About half-way through the process, I began to think that this was all well and fine but surely by the time I got to the end I would have to make some compromises. I doubted that the final stones would actually reflect the rune they were representing, but I kept on going. What else could I do? My pulse quickened when I was at the third to last stone, then the second to last and they each still seemed perfectly suited. Could this really be happening? Then I looked down at the last stone left in front of me. It was an odd shape whereas all of the others had been much more oval. I thought that it seemed like the odd stone out. Then I looked down at my book to see which rune it would be assigned. It was intended to be the blank rune—the odd one out. I laughed out loud and shook my head as I accepted that the whole process had been guided by spirit, right from picking the stones up off the beach in the first place. My new rune set truly was a gift and was already speaking clearly to me.

{21}
renewal

Each night, when I go to sleep, I die.
And the next morning, when I wake up, I am reborn.
Mahatma Gandhi

One thing is clear, the more you are able to change the way you think, the more you will change the story of your life. Don't head into this journey unless you are prepared to deal with change. If the thought of the known structures of your life falling to pieces around you leaves you terrified and unable to cope, this may not be the journey for you right now. The only way for the new story to take place is for the old story to end.

Sometimes we feel so great about our lives, like everything is on course and the change we seek is so imminent, then we walk into our homes or jobs or out onto the street and something happens that we didn't see coming, but is exactly what is needed for that desired change to happen. It feels like being hit by a truck. You were feeling so good and confident that you could handle whatever was coming. Now it feels like someone is sitting on your chest and you're not sure what to do.

It may seem like there are far too many details to work out and you don't know where to start, but remember that you are not alone and the universe is playing a huge part in what is unfolding before you. The details are being taken care of while you ground yourself in gratitude and anticipate the celebration to follow. Know that everything that needs to happen can happen with ease and grace if you stay in your heart and pay attention to the wisdom that resides there.

You have found the place inside of yourself that trusts and knows that the feeling of fulfillment you seek, already exists. Relish fulfillment and let the details of your life fall into place around you. Follow your instinct with the opportunities that are presented and keep doors open. Allow yourself to take comfort in your thoughts.

Love the part of you that is doubting. Give it reassurance that everything will work out. Love the part of you that is overwhelmed. Take a hot bath or go for a walk in nature. Give yourself the chance to feel what you feel, love it and let it transform into confidence and belief that you are such an amazing, powerful being. You are so powerful that you have brought about these significant changes in your life. This is what you wanted. Don't back down now. Even if you are a little concerned that events aren't unfolding exactly how you wanted them to, know that they are unfolding for the highest good of all and that the universe is scheming to make your life fantastic.

As a baby is born, leaving the safety of the womb and travelling through the birthing canal, we too must be prepared to leave the safety of what we have known, take courageous steps forward through the tunnel and emerge at the other end with a whole new beautiful life ahead. We have found that everything we need is inside of us. There are no questions we can't answer if we listen to our true, inner voices. We have practiced feeling joy and gratitude so they are now a part of our daily existence. Even when dark clouds begin to roll in, we know that the sun is still there shining and that the stars remain to guide us. The whole universe exists within us, just as we exist within it.

Remind yourself that there are no problems, only opportunities. Trust that the opportunities are ones that will set you in tune with your unique, creative talents and allow you to express yourself in the highest way possible. Don't aim to be mediocre. Aim to bring healing and balance to the world. Aim to bring all that is beautiful and exciting within yourself out into reality.

It may not seem obvious at first how what we are doing is actually going to change the world. The outward effects may seem minimal. Perhaps no one is even noticing what we are doing, but every action has a reaction. If you are doing the inner work of regaining control of your thoughts and living in a state of harmony and gratitude, that alone is enough. However you are spending your days, even if at times it seems futile, is less important than how you are treating yourself. If you are pumping out manufactured goods, you have the opportunity to connect with the consciousness of those goods and thank the Earth for her contribution. If you put your love into everything you make or do, people will receive it and that alone will change the world. Find your love and share it!

Like the snake sheds its skin, be prepared to undergo a transformation. It may seem scary at first, but go forth knowing that your new skin is already formed underneath and what you are shedding has served its purpose and is ready to be released. Life is an endless cycle of destruction and rebirth. Be willing to let go and flow and you will be amazed by the new opportunities that come your way.

We use the spiritual energy that flows through us to be instruments of change. It makes sense that when we are allowing all of the unseen forces to work, we will be creating higher forms of beauty. We will be materializing love. We will be breathing in pure light and exhaling fantastic creations, be it a child, a work of art, or a great business idea.

This is the time to employ all of the newfound skills you have practiced. You need to ground yourself, breathe deep, and keep believing. This is the turning point where the cup you have been filling up is now overflowing and the effects will not go unnoticed in your life. No matter how much you want to go back to thinking that your life is out of control, back to the thinking that has kept you safe but stagnant for too long, you can't. You have had too many glimpses of your real creative power to give into the lure of self-pity.

In the matter of acting like what we intend to manifest has already come to pass, before it actually has, what we're really going for is the feeling of excitement. It's kind of a "fake it until you make it" concept. The more we practice feeling thrilled, the more we will draw experiences toward ourselves that bring us excitement. When was the last time you felt really energized about something? Take the time to remember all of the details and let yourself relive the feeling of wanting to burst with giddiness. Jump around the room and do a little dance, if that's what you're compelled to do. Let loose and let the feeling of the moment overwhelm you.

Now, remember that it is within you to feel excitement. You don't have to wait for something to happen in life to take you to that place.

It's like being an actor, draw the emotion out of yourself in order to create the character and the scene. Practice being excited about little things throughout your day. Be excited for other people and the wonderful things that are happening to them, whether you know them or not. Let it be a reminder that everything is possible and your life is changing in every moment. Even if there's nothing you can think of to be excited about, be excited anyways. Pump yourself full of positive thought energy.

Children manage to get so excited about life because experiences are all new for them. They have a beautiful innocence that hasn't been quelled. At what point do we stop shrieking with joy on the swing set? At what point do we stop swinging, all together? If you're having difficulty finding the part of you that remembers how to be excited about life, force yourself to do something you've never done before. Even nervous excitement is excitement. The nervousness comes from entering into the unknown, the place where change take place. Act like you're a stranger in town on vacation and see everything through new eyes. Intend for lovely surprises to happen to you each day. When you are open to giving and receiving creative life energy, the universe will create new experiences for you. Believe that you will experience joy and you will.

Once we have become really good at something and we know it in our hearts, we may experience the feeling that we ought to be sharing what we do or know with others. Others will be empowered by our successes. By openly sharing ourselves, we are encouraging others to recognize their own potential. As we outwardly express confidence, we create an environment for the people around us to also believe in themselves. This is one of the greatest gifts we have to share—the ability to empower others.

What are your feelings about success? How do you personally determine whether something or someone is successful or not? Are you ready to be successful? Take some time to think about what the new and successful you will be like. What will you wear? How will you talk? To whom will you be talking? Where will you go on holidays and how will you spend your money? What repercussions will your success have for everyone else? How will it make the world a better place? If you're getting frustrated because it feels like you're doing everything right but success still isn't coming, it may be because you have a hidden fear of victory. It's possible that you're afraid of success changing your life so dramatically that you won't be comfortable anymore. Perhaps your friends will no longer fit into your world or you'll have to move. Try to get clear on your deepest beliefs about success. There may be some more conditioning for you to clear before there is an opening for victory to come your way.

Often when we're waiting to see how something's going to turn out, we're subconsciously preparing ourselves for disappointment. If it isn't our turn to receive, we don't want to be completely devastated. Unfortunately, this is attracting the energy of disappointment, so we're actually sabotaging ourselves. Perhaps, deep down, we believe that we don't really deserve to receive. Perhaps we are concerned that by us receiving, someone else will go without. The trick is to understand that there are endless parallel universes, all of which are filled with abundance, so there is no need for anyone to ever be without. If you are afraid of disappointment, then you are attached to a specific outcome. Allow the energies of creation more leeway than that. Allow them to throw in surprises. Instead of preparing yourself for disappointment, prepare yourself for the excitement of knowing that something totally amazing is about to unfold.

When you start to feel the quivering inside like a blissful moment is about to happen, dive in with wild abandon. Don't let any part of your being hold you back from experiencing a peak moment in life. Waves come and go and life is too short to drown in fear. Allow yourself to be swooped up by the experience, knowing that you earned it by allowing the expression of your highest self. The feeling of bliss is always there for you to ride. It will become obvious when you are living in the moment—no regrets from the past and no expectations for the future.

What an exhilarating moment it is when you realize you are getting what you intend. It can be a crazy, scary feeling to glimpse your own co-creative power. Opening your eyes in the morning and feeling blessed is a new feeling. Indulge in it. Take this new you out for tea and enjoy the company. Don't fear that you won't be able to sustain what you have going on. You have all of the tools and connections you need to navigate your way through your own story without fear.

As I write this book and pull all of these thoughts out of my head and onto the page, making them concrete, it's no wonder that I am recreating my own story at the same time. How reassuring it is to be able to look at my own advice at a time when I need it the most. My daughter and I have been living on a farm with my boyfriend and his two daughters for seven years. A year and a half ago, we stopped being boy-

friend and girlfriend, but I remained living in the house as the nanny, for the sake of the children. They are all homeschooled and we wanted to try to keep it that way. Certainly there were trying times. As my daughter was wanting to try public school, I had been entertaining the idea of moving into town. The thought of leaving the other two children, who I had raised as my daughters, put me into turmoil.

I took the opportunity to housesit in town for a friend during the last week of August. It was a perfect mini-vacation for me. I spent lots of time writing and playing music and went back to the farm feeling refreshed.

The night I arrived back, after having spent the day writing about the structure of our old lives having to collapse so a new life could unfold, my ex-boyfriend informed me that he wanted me to leave the house, preferably that night. There was a cabin on the property I could use until I came up with something else. I couldn't believe what I was hearing. I hadn't seen it coming at all. Yes, I had entertained the idea of leaving for some time, but I had assumed it would be on my terms! I convinced him that he should let me stay out the week to pack my stuff and get organized.

The next day I went house hunting in town. A friend who was moving away for a year had a delightful, little house with a beautiful garden, right beside the lake. Months earlier, I had dreamed I could live in her house, but it was just a dream. She had rented the house to someone else a few weeks earlier, but he had backed out so she relisted it the day I went looking. The house was mine. If I had looked two weeks earlier, it wouldn't have been. If I had looked a month later, it wouldn't have been. If my ex hadn't kicked me out of the house on the exact day he did… Apparently we can't really change our thoughts without changing our lives. The universe is always listening. When we believe it's all possible, our dreams can't help but come true.

{22}
astuteness

*The cosmic spirit is given to us
in order that we may analyze, weigh,
and clarify things in us which nettle us,
or which we are outgrowing.
Or trying to reshape.*
Thornton Wilder

Isn't it amazing that as we find new ways to see our lives unfold, the truth becomes so much more obvious? Our new experiences begin to back up our new beliefs until there isn't room for doubt any more. As more and more moments happen in your life, reinforcing the notion that what you believe really does create your reality, you are able to expand your imagination and reach for greater and greater heights.

The more in tune you become with all life around you, the more you know that you are an integral part of it all and that whatever you choose to create in your life will have impact on all life. As you listen to the voice of your spirit and the spirit of nature, you can't help but accept that there are many different layers of consciousness that are all interwoven to create the fabric of life.

You can look back on your life now and see how your beliefs have created your path. With an open heart, it becomes clear where you still have some fine tuning to do and where you are truly fulfilled and living in sync with your higher self. There is no need to judge your past as being successful or not because you understand that it has successfully led you to where you are right now. You are on a journey that is perfect in every moment.

Stored anger is a thing of the past. You have forgiven yourself for holding onto all of those stories and allowed your emotions to be released, freeing your body and your mind. The walls you built up between yourself and other people have been dismantled. You've discovered joy in taking a heart felt interest in other people's lives, helping them to feel confident and celebrating successes with them. You are no longer judging yourself, but have found the voice in your head of your own best friend.

Now you are able to judge the right course of action. With a clear mind and discerning eye, you are able to recognize truth, opportunity, and distraction. You make decisions based on wisdom rather than perceived obligations, knowing that there is no good and bad and that there are no problems. There are challenges, to be sure, and there will always be people who choose to live their lives differently than you do, but you are able to accept that this is all a beautiful part of this thing we call life.

You are courageous in a whole new way as a seeker of truth. When opportunity knocks, you open the door with confidence and excitement. You know that whatever happens, it is part of you creating a great story for yourself—the kind of story that is worth sharing because it inspires others, the kind of story that is blended perfectly to make the world a better place.

You hear the truth behind other people's words and you respond compassionately, recognizing that their way of doing things is not what you want for yourself but is where they are at right now. Your own words are spoken from a place of understanding—a heart centered place—to help others connect to their own higher selves.

You know when to act and when to stay still. You know when to let go of your "plan" and just let life unravel before you. You are learning how to align yourself with the people and forces that are an integral part of your journey, feeling blessed by their encouragement. It becomes more and more obvious what benefits you and what lowers your vibration.

All of the information that comes your way is valued, and you are able to pick up on signs and bits of wisdom that are presented to you in every way, shape, and form. The beauty of the blooming flower reminds you that you, too, are the flower in all of its glory. The song of the bird takes your mind to a place where you can understand things that previously eluded you. The words you hear on the radio speak directly to your heart and you know that they are a message meant to inspire you.

You are choosing the words of your story like a master now. Neither the oppressor nor the victim, you are the hero who smiles. Knowing that there is no challenge you cannot find a unique way of facing and knowing that you walk with pure spirit inside of you, you exude confidence and feel peace and joy in your heart, all of which leads to wise decision making.

JANET PEARSON

You are an integrated human being. No longer ruled solely by your mind, you take into consideration the feelings in your body, your emotions and the needs of all life around you. You have a grand vision and are able to seize the moments that lead you in the direction you want to go.

Eight months into my first pregnancy, I had a pretty clear vision of what I wanted the birth to be like. It was going to be at home, in the water, with my husband, sister-in-law and midwife present. The lights would be low and there would be lovely music playing. We had the tub ready to be filled and I had set up an altar in the corner of the room to place some flowers, poetry, and other inspiring items. I had a string of beads that had been given to me by my friends at a blessing way. I had been told at my prenatal class that it was important to have a plan, but also to be willing to let it go. The morning that my water broke at 5am, I was feeling confident with my plan. I drew a tarot card to give me encouragement--Discernment. It didn't really speak to me the moment I drew it, but I added it to the altar and carried on.

By early afternoon I was told that I wouldn't be able to go into the tub because my water had already broken. The baby was turned backwards, pressing against my spine, causing extreme pain that no hot water bottle was going to ease. I started throwing up because of the pain. By early evening my midwife informed me that I was going to have to stop throwing up if I wanted to stay at home because some level of something was dropping. If not, I'd have to go to the hospital. I tried my best, but was unable to stabilize myself. By 1:00 am, after 20 hours of labour, I found myself deciding to go to the hospital. My "wise decision" tarot card remained on my altar, now clearly reminding me that it was time to let go of my plan. At the hospital, early the next morning, they gave me an epidural. I'm sure the doctor on duty was prepping me for a C-section, but my midwife was still by my side, determined that I was going to deliver that baby. By early afternoon the doctor said she would be back in a couple of hours. As she left the room, my midwife muttered, "Oh, this baby will be born by then."

Next thing I knew there was someone asking me if it was okay for a group of three medical students who had never seen a birth before to watch me. I was so far away from my plan at that point that I said, "Sure, bring them in." I was ready to push—bright lights, all kinds of people I didn't know and no music. It turned out I was really glad to have such a crowd cheering me on. It gave me strength and courage I didn't know I had. When the midwife told me to reach down and touch my baby's crowning head, nothing else mattered anymore except the new life that I was bringing into the world. My daughter slipped out and was placed on my breast and I was given full understanding that the universe works in mysterious ways. The more I learn to flow with it, the more ease and grace there is in my life.

{23}
artiste

Inside you there's an artist you don't know about…
say yes quickly, if you know,
if you've known it from before
the beginning of the universe.

Rumi

You may wake up one day and realize that your dream from a few years ago is now your life. The changes you once saw as impossible are now integrated. You don't even think in your old terms anymore as you play with your powerful and glorious self. Life is fulfilling and amazing as you flow with nature.

It is natural for abundance to flow into your life and it is natural for you to feel good about yourself and everyone else around you. You were born to shine light into dark places and to be comfortable in the stillness. With no shame, doubt, or despair, you are free to be the award-winning author of your own story. Every moment of your life is a celebration.

Dance with joy, knowing your divine connection and co-creative capacity. You have the ability to bring real change to the world. Your scope now extends beyond your own awareness. Transformation happens naturally with your presence and the world is delighted to have you as a participant.

Your imagination is the seed of new life and you plant those seeds with deep understanding of the possibility of brilliance. You bring your sense of balance and justice to everything you do. Containing everything within you, you are able to draw out whatever energy is needed at the time, with the wisdom of the ages, to make things happen and inspire people. Working with the highest intention of harmony, you are able to shift your perspective as needed.

Now you are the dreamer with the incredible ability to hold a vision and flow with the forces of nature to bring it into being. You are able to interpret the signs for guidance and direction, knowing there is no single path to a destination. Challenges that pop up are no longer obstacles, only new information to process in the grand scheme of things. You flow with what's happening and smile, knowing that it's all good.

Every possible future exists in this moment. Each memory of the past is just one possibility of how life could have unfolded. The only real moment is the one right now that is gone before you can even acknowledge it. The past no longer has any hold on you because you understand its hidden perfection. Just as you are able to write the future, you have rewritten your past in a way that gives you closure and leaves you with a good feeling in your heart.

When you look at the world now, you see the beauty in everything—even what used to leave you feeling sad and hopeless. You recognize that the despair that exists outside of yourself is a reflection of your own despair. You can heal it by loving the part of yourself that despairs. You cause ripple effects throughout the universe that touch the lives of everyone. You become a universal healer by creating change in your life. You are the universe and the universe is you.

You have confidence, knowing you are guided by intuition through difficult times. Your heart connects you to the wisdom of the ages and insight comes from the energetic forces that work through you. There is no more fear of failure because you trust the process.

Big life changes happen with ease now and you welcome the excitement of old structures falling away. You have experienced the place of still emptiness, the womb of creation, and understand its place in the cycle of life, death and rebirth. You are willing to let go of where you are, so you may be true.

You choose your words with care, both the thoughts in your mind and the words you speak. You have experienced that negativity breeds negativity and that compassion and forgiveness heal. The mindfulness you have cultivated is reflected in the health of your body as each breath cleans your cells, brings fluidity to your joints and muscles, and allows the calm in your heart to spread throughout your entire nervous system. You are aware of your body from the tips of your toes to the point of your nose and when something doesn't feel quite right, you are willing to inquire and clear the blocks.

The undermining voices in your thoughts aren't even there anymore. Now you follow your heart and your passion. You've reached a plateau on the journey to ecstasy. When you look up now, there are limitless paths and you know that any of them is yours for the taking.

There is nothing you can't be in your life. There is nowhere you can't go and no challenge you can't face. There is a blank page in front of you. What are you going to write on it? Who are the characters that are going to be there with you and how will you feel? Your life is your own. Your imagination runs free, knowing that everything is possible. That's the bottom line—everything is possible and it is already done. Keep walking towards it, everyday, and experience the legend that unfolds.

Today I stand at the water's edge and let the wind blow right through me. Some days I barely feel like I'm solid anymore—floating around on cloud nine. Looking up at the peak of Mt. Loki, I see myself up there, arms raised to the sky. I know that I am both there and here. I marvel at all of the amazing friends that I have—really talented, vibrant people. They are artists, healers, builders, educators, and parents. They are children discovering all of the finer aspects of life. I think about my daughters and how blessed they are to have so much understanding at such a young age. I know that my Grandmothers are proud of me, going back for generations.

When I close my eyes, I can feel the water washing over my heart, lapping at my shore. It feels poetic just to be at this point in space and time. There doesn't even need to be words.

I'm utterly amazed at where I live. The view is staggering and nature abounds. The river runs clean. I think I must be doing something right for this place to be the reflection of what's inside of me. I set a new intention—may everyone know the joy I feel right now. The sun warms my skin and the pebbles are smooth beneath my feet. I place this thought into the stillness and let it be free.

Thank you. Thank you. Thank you.

medicine bag

BELIEF REPATTERNING
Emotional Freedom Technique - *www.tapping.com*
Z Point Process - *www.zpointforpeace.com*
The Spontaneous Healing of Beliefs by **Gregg Braden** - *www.greggbraden.com*
The Biology of Belief by **Bruce Lipton** - *www.brucelipton.com*

FORGIVENESS
Colin Tipping - *www.colintipping.com*
Ho'oponopono - *www.ho-oponopono.org*

INQUIRY
Louise Hay - *www.louisehay.com*
Byron Katie - *www.thework.com*
Debbie Ford - *www.debbieford.com*

INSPIRATION
Notes from the Universe - *www.tut.com*
Medicine Woman Inner Guidebook by **Carol Bridges**

MEDITATION
Unity breath - *www.spiritofmaat.com/archive/jun1/unity.htm*
Living in the Heart by **Drunvalo Melchizedek**
The One Command by **Asara Lovejoy**– *www.asara.com*

PHYSICAL BODY
Heart Yoga by **Andrew Harvey and Karuna Erickson** –
   www.yogakaruna.com
Anywhere Yoga by **Katya Hayes** - *www.anywhereyoga.com*
Nourishing Traditions Cookbook by **Sally Fallon** -
   www.newtrendspublishing.com
Cleanse and Purify Thyself by **Dr. Richard Anderson** –
   www.cleanse.net

RELATIONSHIPS
Harville Hendrix - *www.harvillehendrix.com*

OTHER
Dr. Emoto (the importance of water) - *www.masaru-emoto.net*
Heart Math - *www.heartmath.org*
Perelandra Muscle Testing - *www.perelandra-ltd.com*
The Four Agreements by **Don Miguel Ruiz** –
   newagreementsforlife.com

ABOUT THE AUTHOR

Happy to call the Kootenays home, Janet Pearson is gardener, knitter, mother, teacher, writer, cook, dancer, snowboarder, herbalist, poet, musician, actor and mountain girl. She prefers to play with wonder, follow whispers in the wind, and bring beauty to the world.

Visit the author on-line at www.janetpearson.ca.

www.ingramcontent.com/pod-product-compliance
Lightning Source LLC
Chambersburg PA
CBHW071712090426
42738CB00009B/1755